Shutterstock

THIS ENGLAND ANNUAL 2022

Celebrate the best of England

Events • People • Places • Views

Boats in Weymouth Harbour, Dorset

Welcome

Hello, and a very warm welcome to your *This England Annual* where we look ahead to 2022, a year in which we fervently hope things will get back to some sort of normality.

As well as our super-useful guides to each season's great events and anniversaries, we also have an array of tempting features. James Hulme praises the charms of a steam train. Linda Barrett celebrates the choreographed brilliance of the Red Arrows and the thrill it gives when you hear that distinctive roar overhead. But it's not all planes and trains.

Rebecca Franks tells the story of the nation's favourite melody *The Lark Ascending* and Amanda Hodges pays tribute to the comedic genius of the Two Ronnies. There's plenty more, too, including pancakes, chocolate, horticultural heroes and Wimbledon. Enjoy!

Angela

Angela Linforth, Editor.

CONTENTS

WINTER TO SPRING

SPRING TO SUMMER

30

48

16

50

44

90

68

Cover image: Rye, East Sussex. Credit: Shutterstock
Back cover: Leighton Moss Nature Reserve. Credit: Shutterstock

Spring Awakening

by D M Howlett

Now the bittersweet of morn;
Frost like dew bedecks the thorn
Of eglantine and hawthorn bough.
The glade lies silent as a song
Within a heart yet still to sing.
Only the sunbeams' glancing form
Breathes the breath of life and spring.
Now sapling trees stir from within,
All buds rise greening to the sky.
And in this corner of the wood,
The cold of winter passes by.

Shutterstock

Beautiful snowdrops in a sunny winter forest

WINTER TO SPRING

Events of the season, England's best nature reserves and take a trip on a steam train >

WINTER TO SPRING

Katherine Sorrell on the top events from January to March, plus anniversaries of the season

JANUARY 2022

LONDON NEW YEAR'S DAY PARADE

The capital kicks off each new year in style with a parade that's billed as "the world's greatest street spectacular", and in 2022 promises to feature more than 10,000 participants from the USA, UK, Europe and beyond. It starts at noon at Piccadilly Circus and winds its way, via Pall Mall and Trafalgar Square, to a grand finish in Parliament Square. **lnydp.com**

London's New Year's Day Parade is a vibrant street spectacular

WHITTLESEA STRAW BEAR FESTIVAL

A man wrapped in a coat of straw makes quite a sight in the town of Whittlesea, Cambridgeshire.

It's the revival of an ancient tradition that's linked to Plough Monday, though no one quite knows where it originated.

These days there's a three-day festival (which runs from 14-16 January in 2022), with the finale on the Saturday involving more than 250 dancers, musicians and performers performing traditional "Molly", "Morris", "Clog" and "Sword" as the "bear" is led along the street.

It all comes to an end with a ceremonial burning of the costume on Sunday. **strawbear.org.uk**

BURNS NIGHT

Here's to Rabbie!

It's a Scottish tradition that's widely celebrated in England, too – commemorating the birthday (on 25 January) and legacy of the great poet Robert Burns. There'll be whisky, poetry, bagpipes and, of course, haggis. One of the best is at London's Ceilidh Club, which hosts three hours of dancing to a live band and caller. At halftime, the haggis is piped in and Burns's poem, *Address to a Haggis*, is recited. The finale of the evening is a rendition of Burns's most famous poem, *Auld Lang Syne*. **ceilidhclub.com**

HOLLY HOLY DAY

On 25 January 1644 the siege of Nantwich was lifted by Parliamentary forces and, to commemorate the battle, the Cheshire town holds an annual day of celebration – called "Holly Holy Day" because the locals wore sprigs of holly in their hats. As well as a parade and battle re-enactment by troops from the Sealed Knot society, there's live music, refreshments, morris dancing and a wreath-laying ceremony. **battleofnantwich.org**

250 YEARS OF TRAVELLER'S CHEQUES

Before the advent of credit cards, ATMs and pre-paid currency cards, the humble traveller's cheque was the best way to take money on holiday abroad. Though gradually dying out, they are still available, and celebrate their 250th birthday this month, having first gone on sale on 1 January, 1772. Issued by the London Credit Exchange Company, they could be used in 90 European cities.

Remember them?

THE WASSAIL

A wassail to awaken the apple trees

From the Anglo-Saxon phrase "waes hael", which means "good health", wassailing is a traditional custom intended to bring luck. Many local events take place around Christmas and the New Year, usually in the form of groups that visit local properties to sing folk songs and bring good cheer, or an orchard wassail in which evil spirits are banished and the apple trees blessed to encourage the crop.

There may well be a procession, songs and dancing, and a wassail drink. Some National Trust properties hold wassailing events. Also try:

• The Cider Works in Crediton, Devon, where the entertainment includes a wassail play and a fire dance. **sandfordorchards.co.uk**

• Pilgrim Morris perform a wassail around the oldest pubs of Guildford, Surrey, on Twelfth Night each year, singing carols and performing the Guildford Mummers Play. **pilgrimmorrismen.org.uk**

• Carhampton Community Orchard in Somerset, where there is a traditional combination of songs, refreshments and ceremony. **facebook.com/CarhamptonCommunityOrchard**

• Bodmin Wassail: this is a custom first recorded in 1624, in which a group of men dressed in top hat and tails visits Cornish care homes, businesses, pubs and homes, singing songs and collecting for charity. **bodminwassail.uk**

• Bolney apple howling, led by the Chanctonbury Ring Morris Men at Old Mill Farm, Bolney, Sussex, including a torchlit procession and "general hullabaloo". **crmm.org.uk/applehowling.html**

HAXEY HOOD

The Haxey Hood is one of the oldest local traditions in England, probably dating back to the 14th century. On 6 January each year, the North Lincolnshire town takes part in a mass game that's a kind of huge rugby scrum or "sway" with very few rules. The aim is to manoeuvre the "hood" (a two-foot length of strong leather) towards one of the pubs or guest houses in the parish. Around 200 people are in the slow-moving "sway", with another 1,000 or so watching.
wheewall.com/hood

DESERT ISLAND DISCS

On 29 January it will be the 80th anniversary of the first broadcast of radio show *Desert Island Discs*. It was presented by Roy Plomley, who also devised the format in which guests choose eight tracks, one book and a luxury to take on their imagined exotic exile. It was initially aired on the BBC Forces Programme before moving to its current home on Radio 4. The first castaway was Vic Oliver, a former music-hall star. More than 3,000 editions later guests have included royalty and rock stars, war heroes and writers, actors and activists, in one of the world's most-loved shows, with many candid and emotional insights revealed alongside the varied music choices.

Roy Plomley with the Beverley Sisters

LONDON ART FAIR

An unmissable opening to the international art calendar, London Art Fair makes a welcome return from 19-23 January, 2022. You will be able to see works from more than 100 galleries presenting the great names of 20th-century modern British art, plus exceptional contemporary work.
londonartfair.co.uk

SLAPSTICK FESTIVAL

If you enjoy the stars of the silent screen – Harold Lloyd, Charlie Chaplin, Buster Keaton and more – you'll love Bristol's annual celebration of slapstick. It brings together guest comedians, experts and film historians in a passionate and hilarious celebration of classic silent and physical comedy.
slapstick.org.uk

Comedian Harold Lloyd

>

FEBRUARY 2022

GRIMALDI CLOWN SERVICE

Joseph Grimaldi is known as the king of clowns, and scores of professional clowns of all descriptions, in full costume, pack the pews for this popular annual service (on the first Sunday in the month) at All Saints Church in Haggerston, London.
clownsinternational.com

CANDLEMAS

The Christian festival of Candlemas, which commemorates the presentation of Christ at the Temple, takes place on 2 February each year. At Yorkshire's Ripon Cathedral, more than 7,000 candles are arranged in alcoves and in intricate designs on the floor, illuminating its architectural glories.
riponcathedral.org.uk

HURLING THE SILVER BALL

The St Ives Feast Day, on the first Monday after 3 February, starts with a civic procession for the blessing at the St Ia Well near Porthmeor Beach, followed by one of Cornwall's most ancient traditions: the "hurling" of a silver ball. In this boisterous game, participants attempt to win the cricket-ball-sized ball from each other around the town (and sometimes in the sea). Whoever returns the ball to the mayor on the steps of St Ives Guildhall on the stroke of midday receives a silver coin.
stivestowncouncil-cornwall.gov.uk/news-and-events/st-ives-feast-day

A NEW WORLD LAND SPEED RECORD 95 YEARS AGO

Ninety-five years ago, on 4 February, 1927, Sir Malcolm Campbell set a new world land speed record at Pendine Sands in Carmarthenshire. Driving the Napier-Campbell "Blue Bird", he achieved 174.22 mph, which remained the UK land speed record until 1969. The current holder of the outright world land speed record is Andy Green, who broke the sound barrier by driving his ThrustSSC at an extraordinary 763 mph at Black Rock Desert, USA, back in 1997.

Malcolm Campbell testing his car prior to breaking the record

THE LONDON CLASSIC CAR SHOW

For anyone who appreciates the fine lines of a classic car there's nowhere to be other than London's Olympia, where you can see (and even buy) some of the world's most desirable vehicles, and celebrate iconic marques from decades past.
theclassiccarshowuk.com

The Queen's first public engagement, 1952

70 YEARS SINCE HM THE QUEEN ACCEDED THE THRONE

In a year of 70th anniversaries for the Royal Family, 6 Feb, 1952 is one of the most significant: it is the date that Elizabeth II succeeded to the throne on the death of her father, King George VI. She was on a tour of the Commonwealth at the time, and that night was staying at Treetops, a Kenyan game-viewing lodge overlooking an elephant waterhole, enjoying a short break in royal duties. Because of the remote location, it was some time before the news reached the royal party, and it was only broken to the Queen by Prince Philip the following day. British hunter Jim Corbett, who was staying at Treetops at the time, wrote in the visitors' book: "For the first time in the history of the world, a young girl climbed into a tree one day a Princess and after having what she described as her most thrilling experience she climbed down from the tree next day a Queen."

And later that year in evening dress

DARK SKIES FESTIVALS

National Parks remain some of the darkest places in Great Britain, and our star-studded skies are celebrated at winter festivals in the North York Moors, Yorkshire Dales, Cumbria, Northumberland and the South Downs. **darkskiesnationalparks.org.uk**

Dark Skies on the North York Moors

JORVIK VIKING FESTIVAL

Jólablót was a raucous Viking celebration of the arrival of spring and the end of winter hardships. Now taking place in half term in York, this annual family-friendly festival is the largest of its kind in Europe. Get your helmet ready and listen to Norse sagas and stories, meet "real" Vikings and learn about their crafts, visit a reconstructed village and watch spectacular battle re-enactments. **jorvikvikingfestival.co.uk**

DERBY CAMRA WINTER BEER FESTIVAL

Dubbed the "Real Ale Capital" of Britain, Derby hosts this four-day festival in one of its iconic railway buildings, the world's oldest Roundhouse. The annual celebration of real ales, lagers and ciders has live bands and tutored beer tastings, with visitors exploring the city as they sample the produce of its respected microbreweries. **derby.camra.org.uk/winter-beer-festival**

KESWICK FILM FESTIVAL

Cumbria's answer to Sundance, this acclaimed festival offers a programme of the best of world and independent cinema, with everything from blockbusters to thought-provoking documentaries, plus retrospectives and special guests. **keswickfilm.org**

SIX NATIONS RUGBY

England's home matches for the Six Nations Championship, the oldest international rugby tournament in the world, take place at London's Twickenham Stadium in February and March. **sixnationsrugby.com**

England v Ireland

CHINESE NEW YEAR

The Chinese Year of the Tiger begins on 1 February, 2022, and celebrations will take place in major cities around the UK, including London, Manchester, Liverpool, Birmingham, Leeds and Southampton. The capital's celebrations are the biggest outside Asia, and involve hundreds of thousands of people descending on the West End for a host of spectacular free events, including a huge parade, lion dances and a variety of stage performances. The centrepiece parade begins at 10 am in Charing Cross Road, then snakes its way through Shaftesbury Avenue in Chinatown. The fun in Trafalgar Square begins at 11 am. The finale – from 5.45 pm – includes a dazzling pyrotechnic display. **visitlondon.com/things-to-do/event/4733685-chinese-new-year-in-london**

The Chinese New Year in London, a highlight

RHUBARB FESTIVAL

The district of Wakefield in Yorkshire has a long tradition of rhubarb-growing. In what is usually the first major food festival of the calendar year, you'll find speciality market stalls, food demonstrations, family fun, arts and crafts stalls, exhibitions, comedy, live music and special events. And, er, plenty of rhubarb. **experiencewakefield.co.uk**

The Rhubarb Festival in front of Wakefield's Cathedral

MARCH 2022

UK WIFE CARRYING RACE

On a Sunday early in March, this extraordinary event is run over a course of 380m, including water hazards (buckets and water pistols), at Dorking in Surrey. Rules are that males or females carry a "wife", who must be alive, human, at least eighteen years old, can be male or female, and does not need to be the carrier's actual wife. There's a minimum weight, and recognised holds include bridal, piggy-back, shoulder-ride, fireman's, Estonian and Dorking, or reverse Estonian. The winner gets to compete in the Finnish wife carrying championships.
trionium.com/wife

WORLD PASTY CHAMPIONSHIPS AND ST PIRAN'S DAY

In a day of music, comedy, food and fun at the Eden Project in Cornwall, bakers from around the world compete for the crown of pasty champion. This year's event is a 10th anniversary celebration, taking place on St Piran's Day, Saturday 5 March, the national day of Cornwall – when a range of festivities are held around the county. **cornishpastyassociation.co.uk**

THE CHELTENHAM FESTIVAL

One of Britain's favourite horse racing events, the Cheltenham Festival is famous for its lively atmosphere, and in particular the roar from the stands as the tape is lifted to start the first race. The festival, which encompasses live music, shopping and world-class food and drink – and 28 races over its four days (this year from 15-18 March) – attracts some of the world's finest horses and jockeys, with royalty and celebrities in attendance to be seen enjoying champagne and a flutter. It all culminates in Gold Cup Day. **thejockeyclub.co.uk**

EVENTS ON SHROVE TUESDAY

Shrove Tuesday, which falls on 1 March in 2022, is the day before Ash Wednesday and the start of Lent, with the day before known as Collop Monday. There are many traditional customs observed at this time, often centred on using up eggs by making pancakes and letting off steam with boisterous games before the penitential season begins. They include:

- The pancake race at Olney, in Buckinghamshire, now world famous. See our feature on p28.
- "Mob" football matches at Alnwick Castle, Northumberland; Ashbourne, Derbyshire; Sedgefield, County Durham; and Atherstone, Warwickshire. Expect few rules and unusual interpretations of what constitutes a pitch and goal.
- In St Columb Major, Cornwall, a hurling match with a silver ball (like the one in St Ives on Feast Monday in February) is contested between the Townsmen and the Countrymen every year.
- Lentsherd in Clovelly, Devon, in which local children drag tin cans down the village's cobbled street at dusk, making a deafening noise said to banish the devil into the sea before Lent.
- Traditional long-rope skipping, which takes place on Foreshore Road, Scarborough, each year. Children are given time off school and the beachfront becomes a centre for family fun.

CRUFTS

Established by Charles Cruft in 1891, this world-famous event held at the NEC in Birmingham boasts 20,000 canine competitors and has become an essential date in any dog lover's calendar. This year it begins on 10 March, with the grand finale, "Best in Show", on the 13th. Look out for Scruffts (for crossbreeds), the dog hero competition "Friends for Life", and "Discover Dogs".
crufts.org.uk

THE FA CUP FINAL'S 150TH ANNIVERSARY

The Royal Engineers in the First FA Cup in 1872

On 16 March, 1872, the Wanderers became the first winners of the FA Cup, beating the Royal Engineers 1-0 at the Oval in Kennington, London, in front of a crowd of just 2,000, who had each paid a shilling to watch. The contest had been suggested by Charles Alcock, then secretary of the Football Association, to generate more interest in the game, and a dozen clubs entered. The Wanderers were the underdogs, but after ten minutes of play one of the Royal Engineers broke his collarbone (though he bravely stayed on the pitch); five minutes later Morton Peto Betts scored the single goal that took his team to victory. Wanderers, incidentally captained by Alcock, had six future internationals in their side, including Robert Vidal, known as "the prince of dribblers".

75 YEARS SINCE THE THAMES FLOOD

Following an exceptionally harsh winter, in March 1947 melting snow coupled with an extremely high tide and frozen ground caused the 20th century's most severe Thames flood, which affected much of the Thames Valley and threatened lives and livelihoods. Although no one died as a direct result, many residents were displaced and some had to be rescued by the army using punts. Telephones, gas and electricity failed, roads were impassable, refuse went uncollected, and essentials had to be delivered to first-floor windows using ladders on boats and hooks on lines. It was a shocking event which resulted in a major change in government policy regarding flood control.

Thames high water marks

TICHBORNE DOLE

On Lady Day, or 25 March, each year, local people queue up to claim a gallon of flour each from outside Tichborne House in Hampshire, distributed from a large wooden bin. The charity dole is said to have begun in the late 12th century when Lady Tichborne lay dying and Sir Roger consented to provide a charity from as much land as his wife could walk round holding a lighted torch. She managed to crawl around 23 acres before the torch blew out, and prophesied that the House of Tichborne would fall if the charity were discontinued.

ORANGES AND LEMONS CHURCH SERVICE

"Oranges and lemons, say the bells of St Clement's" and the bells of St Clement Danes Church, a Grade I listed, 17th-century Wren church in Westminster, do indeed ring the famous tune. The association goes back to medieval times, when the churchyard of St Clements reached the bank of the river Thames, and cargoes of fruit from overseas were transported through it.

Since 1919, when a special service was organised to mark the re-hanging of the church bells, the church has hosted an annual Oranges and Lemons Service on the third Thursday in March. **stclementdanesraf.org**

WOW LONDON

Each year, to mark International Women's Day on 8 March, world-class speakers, activists and performers come together for WOW – Women of the World festival. WOW is a global movement that's all about events, performances, demonstrations, classes and debates in a fun, diverse and energetic atmosphere, and it's just as welcoming to men and boys as it is to women and girls of all ages and backgrounds. The UK's WOW festival takes place at the Southbank Centre in London. **thewowfoundation.com**

COUNTRY TO COUNTRY

Europe's biggest country music festival takes place each March in London, Glasgow and Dublin, with three days of the world's best and emerging talent in country music performing live on the main stage and more intimate, smaller stages. This year's London event is at the O2 Arena in Greenwich from 11th to 13th March. **c2c-countrytocountry.com**

DISCOVER LINCOLNSHIRE WEEKEND

Every March sees a weekend of free entry to many of the attractions in and around Lincoln, as well as other free activities and special offers. Highlights include rides on Lincoln's open-top tour bus, entry to Lincoln Cathedral, and guided tours of the city. **visitlincoln.com**

THE BIG ONE FISHING SHOW

For fishing fans this is the chance to get your hands on the newest kit at discount prices, as well as advice from the experts. There's also a demonstration theatre (including an indoor lake), offering instruction and entertainment from stars of the sport. It takes place at Farnham on 5th and 6th March, and at Stoneleigh on 2nd and 3rd April. **thebigoneshow.co.uk**

RAPHAEL AT THE NATIONAL GALLERY

The artist Raphael shaped Western culture, capturing in his art the human and the divine, love and friendship, learning and power. This major exhibition of his work, opening at London's National Gallery in spring 2022, is one of the first ever to explore Raphael's complete career, looking at his celebrated paintings and drawings as well as architecture and poetry, and designs for sculpture, tapestry and prints, with loans from the Hermitage, the Louvre, National Gallery of Art, Washington, the Prado Museum, Uffizi Museum and the Vatican Museum. **nationalgallery.org.uk/exhibitions/the-credit-suisse-exhibition-raphael**

Raphael's Madonna

Images: Shutterstock and Alamy

ENGLISH BRIDGES

MATHEMATICAL, CAMBRIDGE

Mairi Hughes pays tribute to a unique 18th-century bridge on the River Cam

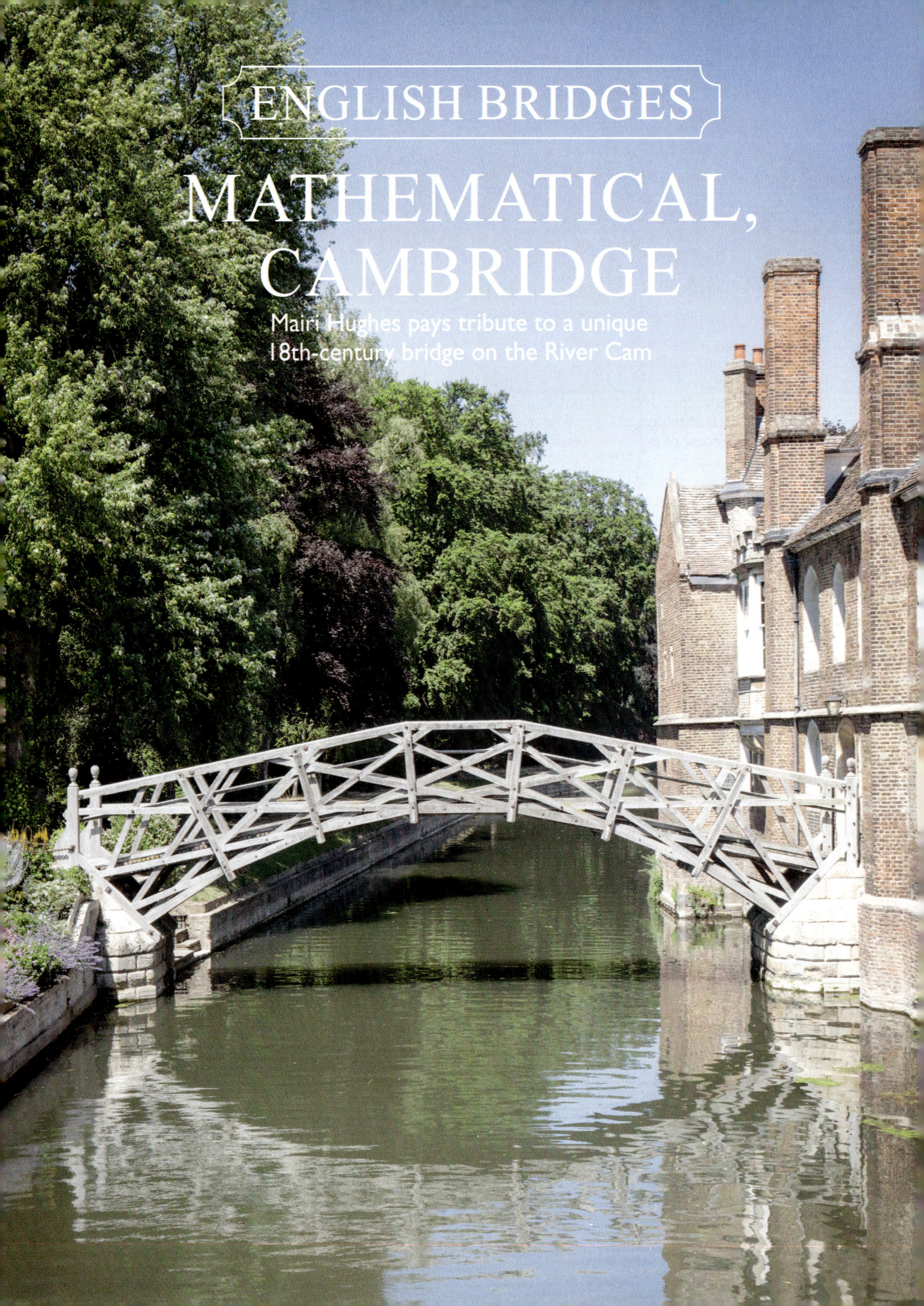

Cambridge Botanic Garden

The Corpus Clock

The Fitzwilliam Museum

IN 1748, English civil engineer William Etheridge drew up plans for what would later become one of the most iconic bridges in Cambridge. The name of the Mathematical Bridge derives from its intriguing structure, which forms an arch despite being made up entirely from straight timbers.

Although this bridge was not the first to use this design in some form, it was considered a triumph of engineering when it first appeared in the city.

The water which flows below the bridge is often inundated with punts filled with tourists. A trip under the bridge provides a fascinating view of the genius of Etheridge's design: the series of short beams of wood which appear to curve round to support the walkway.

However, as impressive as the Mathematical Bridge is, it is not quite as spectacular as the myths surrounding it would have you believe. Local lore claims that the bridge was designed and built by Sir Isaac Newton, and that the design was so ingenious it did not require any screws, nails or bolts to support it.

The story goes that, some years after its original construction, students and scholars from Cambridge University dismantled the bridge to prove that it was in fact free from screws, nails and bolts.

However, when they could not put it back together, they had to add the screws which exist today. While this tale may or may not be true, the bridge has been rebuilt to the same design not once but twice, in 1866 and in 1905.

Cambridge's Queens' College is still in possesion of an old model of the bridge, which is believed to be Etheridge's own model from 1748. This model shows screws at each of the bridge's joints, which would suggest the romantic tale of Newton's bridge is sadly untrue.

The bridge, originally named the Wooden Bridge, runs over Cambridge's River Cam and connects the oldest buildings of the university's Queens' College with its more recent ones. The Tudor buildings on one side of the bridge are some of the oldest on the River Cam, and house Queens' College's President's Lodge.

The Mathematical Bridge is one of the most photographed attractions in Cambridge and draws a great deal of foot traffic. Notably, the Queen followed in the footsteps of tourists when she made use of the bridge on a 2005 visit to Cambridge University.

You can access the bridge through the visitor's entrance to Queens' College on Queens' Lane. Visits cost £3.50 per person (children under 12 go free) and allow you to walk over the bridge and explore the rest of the college. The college is closed to visitors during the examination period from late April until mid-June, and is also often closed for events, so check ahead before you visit.

If you want to get a unique view of the bridge, you can rent a punt from one of the many local punting businesses, or join a punting tour, and view the bridge from underneath!

THINGS TO DO IN CAMBRIDGE

Cambridge Botanic Garden
Cambridge University's Botanic Garden contains over 8,000 beautiful plant species from around the world, which are regularly used by the university for horticultural research. A standard adult ticket costs £6.30. Opening times vary – check in advance of your trip.
Cambridge University Botanic Garden, 1 Brookside, Cambridge CB2 1JE; 01223 336265; botanic.cam.ac.uk

The Fitzwilliam Museum
On a rainy day in Cambridge, seek refuge in the Fitzwilliam Museum, filled to the brim with arts and antiquities. Opened in 1848 to display the collections of Cambridge alumnus Viscount Fitzwilliam, today the free museum displays artwork from Monet, Picasso and Van Gogh.
The Fitzwilliam Museum, Trumpington Street, Cambridge CB2 1RB; 01223 332900; fitzmuseum.cam.ac.uk

The Corpus Clock
If you're passing Corpus Christi College, look out for The Corpus Clock. Designed by college almunus John C. Taylor, the clock was unveiled in 2008. It features the "time eater" creature and is intended to demonstrate the fleeting nature of time.
The Corpus Clock, 58 Trumpington St, Cambridge CB2 1RH; 01223 338000; corpus.cam.ac.uk

Images: Alamy, Shutterstock

Bournville's carillon and school

WHERE ROSES GROW

100 years ago the world lost renowned philanthropist George Cadbury. Brian Conduit heads to Bournville to better understand the man's legacy

LOOKING back on the Cadbury family legacy, it's striking how it all started in such an unassuming way. In 1824 a young Quaker businessman opened a shop in Bull Street in the centre of the rapidly growing industrial town of Birmingham. Selling cocoa, drinking chocolate and tea, there could not have been a more suitable business for a devout Quaker with such products regarded as highly desirable alternatives to alcoholic drinks.

His name was John Cadbury and it was from these unpretentious beginnings that one of the best loved companies in Britain grew. Thousands of us will have happy childhood – even adulthood – memories of Dairy Milk chocolate, mugs of Bournville cocoa, or choosing their favourite from the selection in a box of Milk Tray.

George Cadbury, taken when he was 78

Cadbury's wasn't just a successful company commercially. It was based on strong religious and ethical principles which permeated the whole enterprise and the lives of its employees. These included the provision of pleasant and healthy living and working conditions which, later in the 19th century, resulted in the creation of Bournville, a model industrial village adjacent to the chocolate factory, which was nicknamed "The Factory in a Garden" due to its green surroundings.

But going back, John wanted to branch out into manufacturing chocolate as well as selling it and soon moved into a nearby warehouse. Then, in 1847, he moved into larger premises in Bridge Street, still in the centre of Birmingham. The business had its ups and downs, and problems intensified when John began to suffer bouts of deep depression following the death of his wife in 1851. In the end he relinquished control, handing over the business to sons George and Richard in 1861.

Richard, John's second son, had already been helping his father to

Images: Alamy, Shutterstock

run the firm. George, his younger brother, had been apprenticed from the age of 16 to Joseph Rowntree in York to learn the trade, but his father's depressed state meant that he returned to Birmingham before completing the placement. Though the duo were able, resourceful and even visionary, they still struggled and at one stage had to dig into their own pockets to keep the business afloat.

It wasn't until George went on a visit to Jan Van Houten in Holland that their fortunes changed. George heard that the Dutch chocolatier had devised a way of removing much of the unwanted fats from the cocoa and returned with one of Houten's fat reducing machines. It enabled the brothers to produce a better form of cocoa, advertised under the slogan "Absolutely Pure, Therefore Best", and set the business on the road to success.

The brothers had a vision, based on their Quaker beliefs, that wealth creation should be used not just for the enrichment of the factory owners but also for the benefit of the workers and the community. Both were shocked by the terrible conditions in which most workers in Birmingham's centre lived and set about creating a greener, healthier environment for their employees. "No man ought to be condemned to live in a place where a rose cannot grow," George avowed.

George and Richard came up with a plan to build a new factory on a rural site away from the urban smoke, disease and slums. Finally they found a piece of land that seemed just right: four miles to the south of the town centre and with excellent transport links next to a canal and railway line.

This move to "Bournville" began in 1879. The name came from an amalgamation of Bourn, the stream (Bourn Brook) that flowed through the area, and Ville, the French word for town, thought to be suitable as French chocolate was widely admired at the time.

Initially there were only a few houses built for staff after the factory was established, with most of the workforce still living close to Birmingham's centre and travelling out to the new village. Ever driven, the Cadbury brothers instigated a comprehensive housing programme in 1895 but Richard was not to see its fulfilment. He died from diphtheria in 1899, leaving George to continue the project alone. Richard's unexpected death made George redouble his efforts to complete what had been their shared dream – the pair had always been close.

Fortunately George was the ideal man for the task, and under his guidance Bournville was carefully planned along the lines of a traditional English village. The green was to be the hub surrounded by houses, shops and communal buildings providing educational, religious and leisure facilities. He stipulated that one-tenth of the village should be "laid out and used as parks, recreation grounds and open space" and was insistent on the provision of good quality housing, ensuring each house had enough garden space to grow food.

"We must destroy the slums of England or England will be destroyed by the slums . . . We must not house our workers in a vile environment and expect their lives to be clean and blameless."

Bournville was a landmark achievement in coal-hearted industrial England, but not alone. Roughly contemporary with a similar model village that Lord Leverhulme was creating adjacent to his soap factory at Port Sunlight on the Wirral, it also coincided with the birth of the Garden City movement. Pioneered by Ebenezer Howard at Letchworth and Welwyn Garden City, the movement had a similar emphasis on plenty of green open spaces.

The Cadburys had a reputation as good and well meaning, if somewhat paternalistic, employers. The company provided an extensive range of sports, medical and educational opportunities, set up various clubs and societies and organised coach outings. Spiritual

Drumming up interest in Milk Tray, 1958

Advertising Dairy Milk bars, 1929

Even Bournville's rugby team drank cocoa! >

A Quiet Corner at Bournville, from a selection of illustrations of the village, 1892

needs of the villagers were also catered for; despite the family's strong Quaker convictions, an Anglican church was built. A village pub, of course, remained out of the question.

George had numerous and widespread philanthropic projects. He donated large areas of the Lickey Hills Country Park on the south western outskirts of Birmingham to the city's people, for instance, and gave a large house in Northfield to the Birmingham Cripples Union in 1907. It was used as a hospital, today known as the Royal Orthopaedic Hospital.

Such projects never distracted from business, however, and George was instrumental in developing Cadbury's into a global success story. One of the most successful ventures was the introduction of the Dairy Milk bar. Several chocolate companies both in England and abroad had been experimenting with a milk chocolate bar but in the 1890s the Cadburys landed on a recipe similar to the leading Swiss chocolate bars of the day. Then, in 1905, Cadbury's revealed Dairy Milk, a creamier full milk version. By the early 1920s, it had taken over the UK market.

George was aided in his work by a strong and happy home life, and was father to 11 children. He was married twice; first to Mary Tyler in 1872 and, after her death in 1887, to Elizabeth Taylor. In 1913 he celebrated his silver wedding anniversary and to mark the event a grateful workforce raised the money to build the Rest House, which still stands on Bournville Green. He died in Birmingham, his home ciy to which he had contributed so much, in 1922.

After his death the company continued to expand, taking over some of its chief competitors and developing new brands. After a long and at times acrimonious battle, Cadbury's was taken over by the American company Kraft in 2010 for the sum of £1.9 billion.

A plaque on the wall next to the tomb of Sir Christopher Wren in St Paul's Cathedral states "Si monumentum requiris, circumspice": "If you seek a monument, look around you". The same could be said about George's Bournville. Apart from his contribution to the family business, it is perhaps his most lasting legacy, and certainly the most demonstrative of his character. Before its time, the model village attracted considerable worldwide interest and statistics indicated that the health of children living there was considerably better than those living in the inner city.

Bournville can still be visited today and is now also home to the tourist attraction Cadbury World, which opened in 1990, where you can find out about the history of chocolate, the Cadbury family, the village and the company's famous advertising campaigns. The highlight of course is taking a look around the compact village itself. Starting at the triangular, sloping green at Bournville's heart, you'll see the octagonal Rest House, which was modelled on the well-known yarn market at Dunster in Somerset and is now used as the visitor centre for the carillon, one of the finest in the UK, housed nearby.

Shops built in 1905 surround you as well as two medieval houses, originally on other sites but saved from dereliction and re-erected here. They help to reinforce the old world village atmosphere. There's also the Friends Meeting House, Ruskin Hall, originally conceived as a social centre and specialising in arts and crafts, and the junior and infants schools. All these buildings date from the first decade of the 20th century while the Anglican church was completed slightly later – just after World War I.

Walking along some of the roads in the vicinity of Bournville Green is another way to sample the different styles of housing, all far superior to the usual standards of workers' accommodation back then.

Although originally in a rural setting, Bournville has since been engulfed by the expansion of the city and was incorporated into Birmingham in 1911. Despite this, it has managed to retain its unique ethos and village atmosphere. Considering the chief reason for this brings us back to George. Ever far-sighted, in 1900 he set up the Bournville Village Trust to administer the village, oversee its development and preserve its character. By separating the village from the company almost from the start of the project, Bournville fortunately has been able to survive largely unchanged, despite business upheavals within the Cadbury company.

And you've guessed it – you still won't find a pub!

Cadbury World, Linden Rd, Birmingham B30 1JR; 0121 393 6004; cadburyworld.co.uk

Chocolate Quiz

Sink your teeth into our fiendishly difficult quiz

1. Who played the original Milkybar Kid in TV adverts from 1961-1966?

2. What was the tagline of the macho advertising campaign launched for Yorkie chocolate bars in 2002?

3. What were the five facial expressions displayed by Fry's 5 Boys in the chocolate's iconic advertisement?

4. Which much-loved chocolate bar was the sponsor of *Coronation Street* for a decade from 1996-2006?

5. What song featured on the 2007 Cadbury advert starring a gorilla playing the drums?

6. In *Charlie and the Chocolate Factory*, which Wonka chocolate bar does Charlie find his golden ticket inside?

7. Which famous York based chocolatier, born in 1836, is remembered not only for his family confectionery business, but also for his philanthropy?

8. What are Milky Way bars marketed as in the U.S. and Canada?

9. In 2020, a retro edition of Snickers bars hit shop shelves under the chocolate bar's original name. What was it?

10. The ever rising cost of Cadbury's Freddo bars is a frequent source of despair for chocolate lovers. But in 2018, Cadbury reduced the price of Freddos from 30p to what?

11. What inspired the name of much-loved Quality Street chocolates?

12. What is the name of the popular white chocolate which previously featured in Cadbury's Heroes, discontinued in 2008?

13. Creme eggs were originally marketed as Fry's Creme Eggs. When did they first appear on our shop shelves as Cadbury Creme Eggs?

14. What does KitKat's famous slogan suggest we do while we have a KitKat?

15. Which actress and comedian famously claimed Terry's chocolate orange is "not Terry's, it's mine"?

16. Which British chocolate brand has been creating "Chocolate Heaven Since 1911", when the company was launched in Sheffield?

17. What is the name of the converted London chocolate factory which now acts as a theatre?

18. Which Cadbury chocolate bar is named after a Birmingham village?

19. Actor and professional wrestler Mr T appeared in several Snickers adverts throughout the noughties sporting which catchphrase?

20. Which round chocolate snacks were originally named "Energy Balls"?

Answers on page 106

Identify the chocolate...

21.

22.

23.

24.

25.

26.

Images: Alamy

FRIENDS IN HIGH PLACES

Nature comes alive in spring, so venture through these glorious wildlife reserves with the RSPB's Helen Moffat

BEMPTON CLIFFS

Bempton welcomes around half a million seabirds in the spring to begin a noisy breeding season on Yorkshire's steep chalk cliffs overlooking the North Sea.

Special for: Attracting England's biggest seabird colony over the spring and summer months – funnily enough, these precarious cliffs actually provide ideal nesting sites for many different seabirds. Not to mention the spectacular sea views along this lovely stretch of coast.

Spring highlights: Seeing a whole host of breeding seabirds starting to return, including gannets, puffins, guillemots, razorbills and kittiwakes. The grassy clifftops are also great for spotting farmland birds such as skylarks, tree sparrows and corn buntings. Look to the sea for porpoises on calm days.

Something different: The RSPB organises puffin and gannet cruises from May to August. These three-hour sea trips sail around the base of Bempton's 400-foot chalk cliffs allowing visitors a unique view of the tens of thousands of seabirds on the rock face, swooping through the air or in the case of the gannets, plunging dramatically into the sea to fish. *RSPB Bempton Cliffs, Cliff Ln, Bempton, Bridlington YO15 1JF*

The chalk cliffs at aptly named Bempton Cliffs

MINSMERE

Located on the idyllic Suffolk coast, Minsmere has a varied landscape, including woodlands, coastal lagoons and heathland, meaning there's a huge diversity of wildlife to see as well as a discovery centre and wild zone activity area for young families.

Special for: An impressive range of wildlife – almost 6,000 species have been recorded here, from tiny lichens in the dunes to the UK's largest land mammals, red deer. Bitterns, bearded tits and avocets are just some of the multitude of birds to train your binoculars on, alongside otters, a host of moths, butterflies and insects.

Spring highlights: With the weather improving, there will be adders warming themselves in the first of the sunshine, and up high, marsh harriers performing their switchback courtship displays. You can take a 4 x 4 wildlife safari with one of the reserve's experienced rangers to help you spot even more.

"When it arrives, it's literally like someone has flicked a switch," says Paul Green (assistant warden) who tells me he could never tire of spring at Minsmere. "The sounds are incredible from every part of the reserve. Black-headed gulls, avocets and lapwings all noisily calling on the scrape and bitterns booming in the reedbed. Signs of new life are everywhere.

"I've seen so much at Minsmere – rare vagrant emperor dragonflies from North Africa, a cliff swallow from North America – but I still come back to our bitterns. I never tire of watching them and eagerly await the first booming calls of the males in the spring."

Conservation: Work done within the different habitats helps to make the site more attractive for particular species of birds and wildlife.

For example, the heath is managed to benefit nightjars, Dartford warblers, natterjack toads and silver-studded blue butterflies.

RSPB Minsmere, Sheepwash Ln, Saxmundham IP17 3BY

ARNE

Coast, open heathland, ancient oak woodland: Arne has it all and it's a joy following the trails across its varied landscape. The location is nothing short of stunning – set on a peninsula jutting out into Poole Harbour and within the Dorset Area of Outstanding Natural Beauty, there's the feeling of an island in some parts with stunning views and lots of interesting wildlife.

Special for: Arne is actually one of the very few places in the UK to be able to see all six of our native reptiles: adder, grass snake, smooth snake, common lizard, sand lizard and slow worm.

Spring highlights: Just the spot to find the secretive woodlark, as well as Dartford warblers – look out for them on the many gorse bushes around the heathland. Eyes down to find sand lizards and commons lizards, too.

Senior site manager Peter Robertson shares an overview of the season: "Spring at Arne starts really early, with woodlarks beginning to sing in February, adders, smooth snakes and sand lizards sunning themselves on warm mornings from March onwards and a thrum and buzz of insects joining in in April."

RSPB Arne, Arne Rd, Wareham BH20 5BJ >

Walkway at Arne Nature Reserve

Three greylag geese flying low over open water at Old Moor RSPB reserve

OLD MOOR

> In the heart of South Yorkshire's Dearne Valley, Old Moor is a wetland reserve, originally created from subsidence caused by coal mining in the area. Once dominated by industry, the site has transformed into a green and tranquil nature reserve.

Settle down in one of the hides dotted across Old Moor to watch the many wildfowl and waders which call this place home either all year round, over winter or as a resting point on their long migratory flights.

Special for: Family visits. A National Lottery Heritage Fund grant has been used recently to add a number of features, including a new circular trail, family hide and wild play area, where getting dirty is "positively encouraged".

Spring highlights: Great crested grebes performing their courtship dance, brown hares boxing in the meadows and sand martins returning to their nest bank.

"As the weather warms up, I love to see the buds and catkins begin to burst beside our paths and the arrival of our blackheaded gulls who will provide a constant screaming and swirling spectacle through the summer as they raise their chicks," community and volunteer engagement officer Liz Harding says.

RSPB Dearne Valley Old Moor, Old Moor Ln, Wombwell, Bolton upon Dearne, Barnsley S73 0YF

Sally gets a lesson in using the pole lathe as part of a wood-working demonstration

SHERWOOD FOREST

Not just the home of legendary outlaw Robin Hood, Sherwood Forest is also a special place for nature. What we see today is what is left of the huge woodland which once covered much of Nottinghamshire and has been overseen by the magnificent Major Oak for around 1,000 years! This colossal old tree is also the famed hiding place of Robin and his merry men.

Special for: With almost 1,000 oaks aged 400 years plus, Sherwood has the best collection of ancient oak trees in Western Europe, providing an important and rare home for many insects, birds, mammals and fungi as well as amazing woodland walks.

Spring highlights: The Major Oak is in bud and the forest begins to green, with woodland specialists such as wood anemone and bluebells adding colour throughout. Bird song is everywhere, peaking in early May as the migrant birds have returned, including the cuckoo.

"I love the feeling of the forest coming alive in spring, the smell and the sudden spike in energy," says Sally Granger, visitor experience manager.

"Birds are louder and more active, greens re-emerge between the browns, reds and purples, and on bright days the sun's warmth breaks through the branches to dapple the world around you.

"I have lots of wonderful wildlife memories from the forest but my favourite thing is to hear the cuckoo calling, it is pure spring."

RSPB Sherwood Forest, Edwinstowe, Nottinghamshire NG21 9RN

HISTORY OF THE RSPB

The RSPB started out as the Society for the Protection of Birds in 1889, founded by Emily Williamson at her Manchester home as she and a number of other women fought to save thousands of birds from being killed for their plumage. It's hard to believe now, but at that time having an elaborate feather in your hat was considered the height of fashion.

Membership quickly grew and the society was granted its Royal Charter in 1904. A few short years later and campaigning resulted in the passing of the Importation of Plumage act, banning the import of feathers into Britain. Just last year, the RSPB celebrated the centenary of this event.

The charity has grown in the century since the legislative success to include more than 1.2 million members, managing 220 nature reserves around the UK, and has widened its mission to include conservation of all nature, not just birds. Its mission is to save threatened wild birds and other wildlife, to protect, restore and create more wild places, and to inspire people to take action for nature.

Not only are the reserves beautiful green places to spend time in, they also help us better understand some of the essential conservation work the RSPB carries out and why this is good for nature.

Projects such as the recently completed Wallasea Island Wild Coast – a huge and ambitious plan to restore part of the Essex coast – demonstrate on a large scale how looking after nature can help us find ways to fight threats such as climate change and coastal flooding.

The charity is naturally proud to have Her Majesty The Queen as patron.

FRAMPTON MARSH

Considered by some to be one of the best birding sites in England, you're almost guaranteed thrilling close-up views of a huge variety of birds and other wildlife here. The coastal reserve is part of the most mature saltmarsh in the Lincolnshire Wash with habitats made up of wetlands, reedbeds and large freshwater scrapes (shallow man-made pools).

Special for: The Wash is considered the UK's most important estuary, and one of Europe's too, for good reason, offering the perfect conditions for an abundance of wildlife, especially huge numbers of migrant birds.

Spring highlights: Wading birds arrive to breed, including a large avocet colony which you can see on the freshwater scrapes and wet grasslands. Lapwings are nesting and listen out for those unmistakeable skylarks – they are very vocal at this time of year!

"Spring is an amazing time at Frampton Marsh with migrant birds both arriving and departing," says volunteer Lynne Dale.

"There's a change in the guard, with the geese and swans leaving, knowing they will be back, and new beginnings with the excitement of the arrival of breeding and passage summer migrants – some expected, others a surprise. I love the whole thing – the atmosphere, the nature, never knowing what you might see!"

RSPB Frampton Marsh, Frampton Roads, Frampton, Boston, Lincolnshire PE20 1AY

>

Frampton Marsh

An avocet chick

An otter in the reed bed

LEIGHTON MOSS

> Running along the vast shores of Morecambe Bay, some spectacular scenery and wildlife await at this Lancashire gem. Head up the reserve's nine-metre-high Skytower for views over a mixed landscape of reeds, woodland and grassland, with coastal marsh and mudflats beyond, and keep your eyes peeled for otters and red deer.

Special for: The reedbed here is the largest in northwest England, home to breeding birds at this time of year such as bitterns, bearded tits, water rails and marsh harriers.

Spring highlights: Looking out for avocets returning to begin nesting, or large flocks of black-tailed godwits that might stop off on their way back to their own breeding sites in Iceland. Other migrants such as sedge and reed warblers add to the ever-increasing volume of birdsong as spring marches on. There are plenty of newts, toads and frogs to spot around the wildlife ponds, too.

Currently conserving: Recently in the south-eastern section of the reserve more habitats have been created for bitterns; this stocky heron with a dark-streaked, bright-brown plumage, is one of the UK's rarest birds. More eels are also being encouraged, a critical part of the food chain here.

RSPB Leighton Moss, Myers Farm, Storrs Ln, Silverdale, Carnforth LA5 0SW

View from the Skytower at Leighton Moss

We've only covered a smattering of the RSPB's nature reserves of which there are more than 220 to visit. Each runs its own programme of special events, including guided walks and talks, throughout the year. Find one near you at rspb.org.uk/reserves-and-events.

SANDWELL VALLEY

Less than six miles from the busy city centre of Birmingham, it's amazing to discover this lush urban green space, boasting a lake, where lapwing and oystercatchers breed, with walks through the woodland and wildflower meadows.

Special for: Sandpipers that love to stop off for a much-deserved rest here to break up their long migration flights.

Spring highlights: Reed buntings and dunnocks start singing, adding their voices to the growing dawn chorus. Keep your eyes peeled for lapwing chicks, goslings and ducklings on the water, and early butterflies and bees on the spring flowers.

"I love the return of nesting birds and the beginning of new life," volunteer Mick Shillam says. "Sandwell is such a haven for nature – despite the urban environment, we get so many waders here – like little ringed plovers and oystercatchers. Seeing them makes me elated."

RSPB Sandwell Valley, Tanhouse Avenue, Birmingham B43 5AG

Mick Shillam, volunteer at Sandwell Valley

Images: Shutterstock, Alamy, RSPB Images: David Kjaer, Mike Richards, David Tipling, Ben Andrew, Alan Coe

HEARTS OF *Oak*

100 years ago, *HMS Victory* found a new home in Portsmouth Dockyard. Roger Paine reflects on the history of this iconic ship

HMS Victory moved to Portsmouth Dockyard in 1922

BEST known for her role in the Battle of Trafalgar on 21 October 1805, *HMS Victory* is one of the oldest warships still in commission in the world. She epitomises the age of fighting sail, of wooden-walled ships with intricate webs of masts, spars and rigging. Armed with smooth-bore, muzzle loading cannons firing solid iron round shot, these ships were manned by the hardy sailors known affectionately as "Jack Tar".

In December 1758, Prime Minister William Pitt persuaded Parliament to build 12 ships of the line, one to be a first rate of 100 guns. At the time, Britain was at war with France. The war was being fought on an intercontinental scale encompassing America, Canada, the East and West Indies, India and the Philippines.

The design work of the *Victory* was undertaken by Sir Thomas Slade, Surveyor of the Navy. The keel was laid down in the old single dock at Chatham on 23 July 1759. Some 300,000 ft of timber was used in construction of the hull. The overall cost of building amounted to £63,176.3s.0d, equating to approximately £46.5 million today.

In her day, the *Victory* was among the most powerful weapons systems afloat. At the Battle of Trafalgar, the *Victory's* formidable firepower totalled 104 guns mounted on three full gun decks, forecastle and quarterdeck. Her gun crews were trained to fire off a single round every 90 seconds. You can see eight of the original guns used at Trafalgar, including a 24-pdr, displayed on the middle gun deck.

1858 illustration of HMS Victory

Apart from the ship, it is worth recalling the man who will forever be associated with it. Horatio Nelson was born on 29 September 1758. His mother Catherine had a brother, Captain Maurice Suckling, who was a successful naval officer.

At the age of 12, Horatio's father allowed him to join his Uncle Maurice on an assignment fitting out the *Raisonnable* for overseas service. In search of his uncle's ship in Chatham Dockyard in early 1771, he would almost certainly have passed the dock where the *Victory* was being fitted out. The same ship that 34 years later was to be the scene of his heroic death at the Battle of Trafalgar. We can now visit The Orlop Deck, where Nelson was carried after being fatally shot.

It was over a century after Trafalgar that the ship was saved thanks to the Society for Nautical Research and the Royal Navy. She is continuously restored by naval dockyard shipwrights and riggers – some of whom have spent 30 years of their lives maintaining her.

In March 2019, ownership of the ship was transferred to a dedicated *HMS Victory* Preservation Trust established as part of the Museum of the Royal Navy. The Museum's director general, Professor Dominic Tweddle, said, "*HMS Victory* is a national icon. Preserving a wooden warship is a battle – a battle against nature and just as epic, in its way, as the Battle of Trafalgar. To be able to witness how that battle is fought will be a big draw for visitors. We are determined that *Victory* will be open to the public throughout so that they can share in the excitement and even thrills of the restoration story."

She certainly has a legacy of drawing a crowd. Since opening to the public in 1928, *HMS Victory* has received over seven million visitors. Here's hoping she gets even more attention in this special centenary year.

Images: Alamy

OLNEY'S PANCAKE DASH

Shrove Tuesday is the day the women of Olney take on their beloved Pancake Race. Robert Preece finds out more

TUCKED away in Buckinghamshire, the charming market town of Olney is home to a long-standing sporting tradition. Each Shrove Tuesday, local women don their aprons and line up in the town centre, ready to take on the Pancake Race, said to date back to 1445.

Customarily, Shrove Tuesday is not only a day to use up rich foods, often by making pancakes, but also a day of repentance before the commencement of Lent. Olney's famous Pancake Race is thought to have begun with a tardy churchgoer who, being late for a Shrove Tuesday shriving service, ran to the church with her apron still on and her frying pan, complete with pancake, in hand.

Today, local women line up at the town's market place at 11.55am on Shrove Tuesday, pans and pancakes at the ready, and set off at the church warden's ringing of the shriving bell. Tradition dictates that contestants must be women from the Olney area, and must abide by the dress code of a skirt, head covering and an apron.

It's no laughing matter – outrage ensued in 2016 when *Blue Peter* presenter Barney Harwood appeared at the start line to run the race. However, in his blonde wig, apron and skirt he became the first man to run in the competition.

Contestants dash around the 415 yard course, while skilfully balancing their pancakes, to the finish line on Olney's Church Street. And the race doesn't end there. The first woman across the finish line must successfully flip her pancake at the end of the course to secure her victory. Finally, winners must honour custom by making their way to the local church and knocking on the door with their pan, where they are officially declared victorious by the local reverend at the annual shriving service. Traditionally, the prize for the race's winner was a "kiss of peace" from the church's bell ringer.

The tradition has apread and other pancake races in England include Ripon's Shrove Tuesday race, in which clergy from Ripon Cathedral can be spotted racing through the city centre in full clerical garb, saucepans in hand, and the Scarborough Shrove Tuesday festivities, which feature a pancake race combined with a skipping race, which dates back to the early 20th century when local fishermen would sort through old fishing nets and give their children spare ropes to play with.

In 1997, a new custom was born in Westminster when MPs, Lords and journalists ran in the first annual Parliamentary Pancake Race. A team of press take on MPs and Lords in the race around Victoria Tower Gardens, with all contestants sporting aprons and chef's hats. Not only a prime opportunity to have a good laugh at the participants, the race annually raises money for Rehab, a

Olney's Pancake Race dates back to 1445

Olney challenges the US city of Liberal

Barney Harwood tries his hand at pancake racing

Ripon's Shrove Tuesday race

charity supporting brain injury research. Elsewhere in London on Shrove Tuesday, the Inter Livery Pancake Race is hosted by the Worshipful Company of Poulters, welcoming tradespeople from across the city. Participants in this race opt for fancy dress or full regalia (sometimes a combination of both) and take on a route around the Guildhall Yard, clockmakers timing the heats and fruiterers providing fruit for the pancakes.

In 1950, the trend of Shrove Tuesday pancake racing spread across the globe when R.J. Leete of the US city of Liberal, Kansas, spotted a photo of the Olney Pancake Race in the pages of an American magazine and contacted Olney's vicar, the Rev. Ronald Collins. This led to a twinned race in Liberal, in which the women run the same race over the same distance on the same day.

Liberal's Pancake Day has since become an entrenched custom, and the city is now home to the International Pancake Day Hall of Fame, displaying historic saucepans, photographs and medals from the Pancake Race in years gone by, with a gift shop selling official Pancake Race merchandise, including t-shirts, bandanas and whisks.

At the end of the UK and US races each year, times are compared across the Atlantic and an international winner is declared. While tradition was sadly broken last year when the pandemic forced the race to be cancelled, plans for the 2022 event are well underway. Watch this space!

THE OTHER PLACES WHERE SPORT BEGAN

Rugby and Rugby

While a version of rugby known as "harpastum", meaning "seize", was being played by the Romans long before this, the modern game we all know today can be traced back to 1823, and a lawless game of football at Rugby School in Warwickshire, when William Webb Ellis took a chance as he caught a football in his hands and ran with it. This was the birth of "rugby football", now known globally simply as rugby. The game began to spread throughout England as pupils from Rugby School graduated to universities across the country, and took their newfound sport with them.

Ashbourne Shrovetide Football

Football, now the world's favourite sport, is said to have developed in England in the 12th century. However in 17th century Derbyshire, a more niche version of the game was born. The town of Ashbourne hosts a game of Royal Shrovetide Football on an annual basis, played over two days. Two large teams gather in the town centre, where the ball is thrown into the crowd. Players "hug" the ball in a scrum and must push the opposing team towards their goal – the two goals being three miles apart. Play continues for eight hours at a time and the only rules of the game are the ball must be kept out of churchyards and cemeteries, and cannot be hidden in a bag or transported in a car. The "pitch" consists of the entire town and local businesses board up their windows prior to the event!

Much Wenlock and the Olympics

The Modern Olympic games began in a much humbler location than the Olympia of Ancient Greece. Much Wenlock in Shropshire held its first Olympian Games in 1850, founded by Dr William Penny Brookes. The games included football, cricket, athletics and even a wheelbarrow race. The games were open to anyone, with competitors travelling from all over England. In 1861 the Shropshire Olympian Games were founded. Baron Pierre de Coubertin (founder of the International Olympic Committee) visited Much Wenlock around 1890 and it is thought this was the inspiration for the modern Olympic Games which began in 1896.

Stoke Mandeville and the Paralympics

Another Bucks sporting star is Stoke Mandeville, which lays claim to being the birthplace of the modern Paralympic Games. In 1943, Dr Guttman, later Sir Ludwig Guttman, was asked by the British government to establish the National Spinal Injuries Centre at the hospital to treat and rehabilitate injured pilots from World War II. The idea of the games was to encourage patients to get involved in sport to improve their fitness, and no-one was to be excluded however severe their injuries. The first games were held in the grounds of the hospital on 29 July, 1948, the same day the Olympic Games were opened in London. At the 2012 London Paralympics alone, 4,200 athletes took part, and it has perhaps helped shaped other events such as Prince Harry's commendable Invictus Games.

Prince Charles takes on Shrovetide Football

FULL STEAM AHEAD

Leave behind frayed nerves and restricted horizons for a soothing trip at the gentle pace of a steam train, says vintage train fan James Hulme

THE steam hissed. Someone cleared his throat.
No one left and no one came
On the bare platform. What I saw
Was Adlestrop – only the name."

In Edward Thomas's poem, a pause at Adlestrop station represented a moment stolen from life's progress, a temporary suspension of time in which only birdsong can be heard. For another poet and broadcaster, John Betjeman, riding in a train, with its elevated view above the hedges, gave you the dignity and authority of a horse-rider from the 18th century.

The British love of railways – especially in their traditional form – is a peculiar and endearing national trait that we are all ready to indulge once again. Fortunately, a widespread and dedicated preservation movement, almost entirely the work of passionate volunteers, means that you can relive the experience of the steam engine and the branch line at one of many different locations around England.

The age of steam lasted for over 140 years, and this small sample of the many heritage railways you can visit has been selected to represent not only regional variations, but also the historic railway at different evolutionary stages: from its origins in the North East's mining districts to a dainty late-Victorian toy winding along narrow-gauge tracks in rural Devon. They all have the added bonus of running through delightful countryside, with other interesting places to visit close by.

Most heritage railways got their start when British Rail brutally pruned their network in the name of economy back in the 1950s and 60s, making their renaissance and relative prosperity today all the more remarkable. But the pandemic brought immense challenges to their survival and the loss of revenue was devastating. Beyond COVID, another looming threat is the imminent cessation of coal-mining in the UK, denying the lines the vital supply of high-quality Welsh steam coal for which their engines were designed.

Undaunted, all lines reopened in 2021, for these are enterprises that represent our native resilience at its best. All have run emergency appeal funds to cover the loss of 2020's revenue, with a great response from their support base.

While national transport policy dithers, most steam lines have impressive and ongoing expansion plans, and many grow longer with each passing year. In several cases, lines now reconnect to the national network from which they were formerly severed, meaning you can reach them without a car.

Standards of restoration are simply world class – where else can you actually ride in a museum-quality artefact? And in marked contrast to the "big" railway, you will find the staff unfailingly enthusiastic, knowledgeable and friendly. This is the time to show your support and visit our steam trains again.

Opposite: the beautiful Lynton & Barnstaple Railway; Above: departure from Sheringham on the North Norfolk Line; Right: station platform at Sheringham; Below: Woody Bay station on the Lynton & Barnstaple Railway

THE LYNTON & BARNSTAPLE RAILWAY

Included for the heroism of its endeavour as well as its captivating charm, the L&B does not currently reach either of the towns for which it is named. Climbing from sea level to the edge of Exmoor, the line was promoted at the end of the 19th century by prominent Lynton resident and publishing millionaire Sir George Newnes. Because of the vertiginous terrain, it was constructed to the narrow gauge more usually associated with lines to Indian hill stations and Welsh slate quarries.

The tenacious L&B had a famous charm that drew visitors from far and wide, with tiny locomotives and carriages winding up into the hills at a leisurely 12 miles an hour from the Taw Estuary to the exclusive resort perched high on the cliffs above the Bristol Channel. Considered quaint even by the standards of the early 20th century, the line did not escape the attention of the Southern Railway accountants and was closed in 1935.

The revival of this sleeping beauty in the 21st century is remarkable; with strategic foresight, enthusiasts have successfully purchased segments of trackbed and surviving station sites, with the first services recommencing on a mile of track at Woody Bay in 2004. The carriages are heavily restored originals retrieved from a variety of sources, while the delightfully diminutive locomotives are faithful replicas of those built for the line in 1898. The attention to detail is second to none, making the railway, in its glorious setting of rolling hills and coastal vistas, a fabulous place to spend some time. The cheerful drivers might even let you inspect their gleaming footplate if you display a suitably respectful interest.

THE NORTH NORFOLK RAILWAY

Nothing beats a steam journey to the sea. The Midland and Great Northern Joint was built late in the railway age, enterprisingly connecting the industrial cities of the Midlands with the coastal resorts of Norfolk, specialising in holidaymaker traffic along with a lot of fish. >

Top: Re-enactors on the Severn Valley Railway; Above: the Arley signal box; Bottom: the Tanfield Railway museum

> Something of a meandering system, it lost ground to its more direct rival, the Great Eastern, and after years as a backwater quietly closed in 1959. A tiny fragment was preserved, now linking saucy seaside Sheringham with the genteel market town of Holt, and offers a flavour of the time when holidays for the majority meant packed summer Saturday specials, austere boarding houses and invigorating dips in the North Sea.

If you like the smell of salt air mingled with burnt coal, and the prospect of the best fish and chips on a platform seat, then this is the line for you. Alight at Weybourne for a walk up to the heath, from which railway, coastal marshes, pines, windmill and sea all feature in a classic Norfolk panorama.

THE SEVERN VALLEY RAILWAY

The legendary Great Western Railway, the brainchild of Isambard Kingdom Brunel, commands a special following, and this particularly scenic GWR branch through pretty Midlands countryside was a plum choice for preservation when closed as uneconomic in the 1960s.

Proximity to the mighty engineering base of the West Midlands means that the railway has never suffered from a shortage of skilled volunteers. Today, this workforce also includes a new generation of steam drivers and fitters being trained up through an apprentice scheme at the line's Bridgnorth workshops, an initiative funded by the line's own charitable trust.

The SVR is considered one of the jewels of the steam railway movement; when torrential rains caused severe landslips in June 2007 and put it out of action, other heritage railways and the general public contributed to the successful £3.8m emergency fund raised to repair the track.

For the visitor, the line's predominantly steam-hauled, chocolate and cream trains are a delight. As well as the line's own rolling stock, its central location means it is regularly visited by special "celebrity" locomotives from all over the country. Stations, signals and bridges over the mighty Severn evoke the spirit of the country branch line, no platform is without its luggage barrows and milk churns, and immaculately dressed signalmen wave from spick and span boxes.

The attractive riverside town of Bewdley is on the route, as is Bridgnorth, a Georgian gem. For a real treat, allow yourself to be tempted to ride in the Observation Saloon, and enjoy a traditional afternoon tea for a very reasonable supplementary fare, with a unique view of the receding tracks thrown in.

THE TANFIELD RAILWAY

The genesis of the railways was not about leisure travel or even passengers, but coal. The lesser-known Tanfield Railway south-west of Newcastle lays legitimate claim to being the oldest in the world, its origins long predating those of George Stephenson's more famous Stockton and Darlington down the road.

The Tanfield "waggonway" was established by a collective of mine owners in 1725, with primitive horse-drawn trucks on wooden tracks to take local colliery coal down to the Tyne; the adjacent Causey Arch, although no longer in use, is the oldest surviving single-arch railway bridge in the world. The locomotives used on the line today are the characterful tank engines once seen in their hundreds on industrial railways.

Under the auspices of the National Coal Board, examples worked into the 1980s, making them popular conscripts for the emergent preservation railways after they were retired. The tiny, beautifully restored coaches give a flavour of the workmen's trains of the past with authentically hard wooden seats – it is perhaps a blessing that the ride, though evocative, is comparatively short.

If you want to see what the mine owners did with their wealth, visit the nearby Gibside estate, now run by the National Trust, where mine owner and railway promoter George Bowes, a notable ancestor of Queen Elizabeth the Queen Mother and our present Queen, lived in aristocratic splendour.

THE KEIGHLEY & WORTH VALLEY RAILWAY

This much-loved line epitomises the spirit of railways in the north of England. Situated at the heart of rugged West Riding, the passing scenery evokes the industrial heritage of the region as well as the wild moorland immortalised in the novels of the Brontë sisters. The route is one of a very few that preserves a branch line in its entirety, saved after its closure in the early 1960s.

Present-day volunteers must have the true grit of railway pioneers to endure the extremes of local weather, however; I remember a cold March day when visitors could hardly be prised away from the blazing warmth of the station fireplaces to board trains.

The railway in its preserved form shot to fame as the main location of the 1970 film *The Railway Children*, starring Jenny Agutter, and fans can still see the various pieces of rolling stock used in the film, as well as the station comically presided over by Bernard Cribbins. A very steep walk up the hill from Haworth station will take you to the famous village, parsonage and church that shaped the lives of England's most celebrated literary siblings.

THE BLUEBELL RAILWAY

The first standard-gauge railway to be acquired for preservation, the Bluebell Railway was established by outraged Sussex residents in 1959 after British Rail controversially closed the useful link between East Grinstead and Lewes (this singular lack of vision now haunts us all in the lack of alternative routes from London to Brighton when the main line is blocked).

Dedicated to the preservation of steam locomotives and authentic rolling stock, the line's reputation as the senior steam railway is justified by its immaculately restored carriages, stations presented in period authenticity, and the largest collection of locomotives outside the National Railway Museum.

Celebrating more than 60 years of triumphant steaming, the toil of volunteers and tireless fund-raising paid off in March 2013, when the link with East Grinstead at the line's northern end was reinstated and the whole town celebrated.

Now once more connected to the national network, you can leave London for the day and enjoy the gentle swaying rhythm of green carriages as they make stately progress through lush verdant countryside. To complete your journey into arcadia, the National Trust's superb Sheffield Park and Garden are just a short walk from the line's present southern terminus.

First-time visitors will feel they already know the principal station at Horsted Keynes; from *A Room with a View* to *Downton Abbey*, it is the go-to location for film and television whenever a steam era railway is required.

Those wanting to indulge their inner Lady Mary can book a trip on the opulent and popular Golden Arrow Pullman dining trains on Sunday afternoons.

Top: Oxenhope station on the Keighley & Worth Valley Railway; Above: the station clock at Oakworth; Below: Bluebell Railway

Images: Shutterstock, Alamy

Butterflies

by Don Austen

Red Admirals, Tortoiseshells and Peacocks,
To name a few.
Purple Emperors, Painted Ladies
Fly near me, too.
Flitting and fluttering midst garden flowers
In balletic flights.
Settling and waving on lilac buddleia –
A pair of Cabbage Whites.
From caterpillar then pupa, they gradually emerge,
Colourful flutterbys that dance, in meadow and in verge.
Orange Tips and Common Blues fill our summer days
As we, enchanted, stand and stare
At their delightful ways.

Shutterstock

Spring flowers under the woodland trees in Norfolk

SPRING TO SUMMER

Events of the season, the magic of Wimbledon and the Red Arrows in action

SPRING TO SUMMER

Katherine Sorrell on the season's anniversaries and best events, sporting and otherwise

APRIL 2022

BATH COMEDY FESTIVAL

This springtime extravaganza of laughs runs for almost three weeks in April at venues around the beautiful Georgian city of Bath. Featuring household names and newcomers alike, the festival's aim is to bring Bath to life with a vibrant mix of stand-up, sketches, film, theatre, writing, art, workshops, music and mystery tours. **bathcomedy.com**

THE BOAT RACE

The annual contest between rowing crews from Oxford and Cambridge universities takes place close to Easter each year on the River Thames between Putney and Mortlake, except for 2021. There are places to watch the race for free along the full length of the course, with some of the best viewpoints being Putney Embankment. **theboatrace.org**

60TH ANNIVERSARY OF THE CROSSING THAT CAUSED CHAOS

In a bid to increase pedestrian safety, a brand-new type of road crossing was introduced to British roads in April 1962. The panda crossing featured black and white triangular markings and a system of flashing lights, some telling drivers to stop and others instructing pedestrians to cross. With road accidents soaring, the aim was to improve upon the simple, uncontrolled zebra crossing (launched in 1951), but the result was, unfortunately for transport minister Ernest Marples, consternation and confusion.

One of the first people to use the new crossing outside Waterloo Station in London said: "That man Marples is up to too many tricks. It's a hairbrained scheme and most dangerous." A week later, the experimental crossings were modified.

The first crossing in 1962

EARTH DAY

Every year on 22 April, Earth Day marks the birth of the modern environmental movement in 1970. As part of a global initiative to help protect and restore the planet, there are actions happening all over England, from beach cleans to teach-ins, which anyone is welcome to join. **earthday.org**

ST GEORGE'S DAY

A feast day of St George is celebrated in England on 23 April, which was possibly the date of our patron saint's martyrdom. The English Heritage festival at Wrest Park, Bedfordshire, is billed as the biggest St George's Day celebration in the

SOLVING HORTICULTURAL DILEMMAS FOR 75 YEARS

Concerned about your chrysanthemums? Trouble with your tomatoes? For 75 years, the BBC radio programme *Gardeners' Question Time* has been there to help. When first aired on 9 April 1947, answering questions from the Smallshaw Allotments Association, it was actually called *How Does Your Garden Grow?*, but the name was soon changed – though the format has remained remarkably similar, with a panel of experts and lots of down-to-earth advice. Over the years the show has answered more than 30,000 questions, and been the guest of a diversity of gardening clubs and other groups, including Leyhill Open Prison, the Palace of Westminster and a nudist club in Wales.

country, including performances, games, battles and, of course, a showdown between St George and his fiery dragon. Salisbury is also well known for its family-friendly event that includes Morris dancing, live music, fair rides and parades. In London there's a huge celebration in Trafalgar Square, Manchester and Nottingham hold lively parades and there are local events up and down the country.
english-heritage.org.uk; london.gov.uk; visitwiltshire.co.uk/Salisbury

SHAKESPEARE'S BIRTHDAY CELEBRATIONS

Shakespeare's birthday is marked every year in his hometown of Stratford-upon-Avon on a weekend close to 23 April. Highlights include a parade, folk dancing and street entertainment, and the laying of a wreath at Holy Trinity Church where the playwright is buried. **shakespeare.org.uk**

TREVITHICK DAY

Engineer and inventor Richard Trevithick constructed the world's first steam railway locomotive, and each year on the last Saturday of April his life and work is celebrated with a festival of free street entertainment in the Cornish town of Camborne. In addition to music, food, stalls and a flower festival, there are two special dances and an impressive parade of vintage steam vehicles. **visitcornwall.com**

MALDON MUD RACE

This mad mud bath/charity fundraiser takes place on a Sunday in late April or early May in the Essex town of Maldon. It draws crowds in the tens of thousands to watch competitors, often in fancy dress, make their way through the thick mud of the Blackwater estuary and back, on a 400m course. Entry to watch in Promenade Park is by donation; huge TV screens capture every moment, and there are stalls, activities and entertainment. **maldonmudrace.com**

THE TUDOR PULL

The Tudor Pull is a springtime ceremonial event in which Thames Cutters and other craft escort the Thames Royal Shallop *Jubilant* and *Gloriana*, the Queen's barge, from Hampton Court Palace to the Tower of London, delivering a ceremonial token to the governor of the Tower for safekeeping. Expect a visual spectacle with much pageantry, flags and colourful regalia. **pla.co.uk/Events/The-Tudor-Pull**

The royal barge, the Gloriana

FRITILLARY SUNDAY

The snake's head fritillary once carpeted the wet meadows of England; now it is a rare sight, found only in a handful of places. One such site is Ducklington Mead, Oxfordshire, the only place in England where it is possible to walk among the flowers – for just one day a year. On Fritillary Sunday the ten-acre meadow is opened to the public, who may also enjoy ploughman's lunches and cream teas, folk dancing, handbell ringing and a large plant stall, including home-grown fritillaries, with all proceeds going to Ducklington Church. **ducklingtonchurch.org.uk**

See these distinctive snake's head fritillaries in Oxfordshire

THE GRAND NATIONAL

The Grand National is best known for the four-mile steeplechase that is the ultimate challenge in jumps racing. However, it is in fact a three-day festival (7 – 9 April in 2022) at Aintree Racecourse in Merseyside, with the first day, Liverpool's Day, a relaxed day of racing and entertainment, while Ladies Day brings some extraordinary hats! In the exciting finale of the Grand National itself, 40 horses and riders jump 30 notoriously difficult fences over two laps of the Aintree course. **thejockeyclub.co.uk**

CUCKOO DAY

The cuckoo fair in Heathfield, East Sussex, is said to date back to 1315, when Dame Heffle (the old name for Heathfield) used to arrive at a gypsy market and release cuckoos for the start of spring. The day includes craft stalls, food and drink, displays and performances, all raising money for Demelza Hospice Care for Children. At Marsden, West Yorkshire, Cuckoo Day encompasses artistic workshops, a craft fair, maypole and Morris dancing as well as a village procession led by a giant wicker-and-paper cuckoo.
facebook.com/hefflecuckoofair1315

BLUEBELL WALKS

A tranquil walk through an ancient woodland carpeted with beautiful bluebells is a wonderful springtime experience. The National Trust and the Woodland Trust have lists of bluebell walks. **nationaltrust.org.uk; bluebellwalk.co.uk; woodlandtrust.org.uk** >

Carriage driving

ROYAL WINDSOR HORSE SHOW

Taking place in the private grounds of Windsor Castle, top equestrian sport on offer includes international show jumping and dressage plus more than 140 showing classes. There are also displays and music from military troops and bands, the much-loved Shetland pony Grand National, and a thrilling theatrical pageant that combines music and horse skills. **rwhs.co.uk**

GOODWOOF

Billed as "the world's most spectacular dog event", Goodwoof is a grand celebration of all things dog, including agility competitions and demonstrations, dog wellness, family fun, and celebrations of heroic canines. Taking place at The Kennels at Goodwood, West Sussex. **goodwood.com/goodwoof**

THE ALRESFORD WATERCRESS FESTIVAL

Watercress takes centre stage in the Hampshire town of Alresford on the third Sunday of May each year, marking the start of the new UK season of the popular peppery superfood. The Georgian market town was built from the riches of the watercress industry, even boasting its own steam railway nicknamed the Watercress Line. The *pièce de résistance* is The World Watercress Eating Championships. The world record for an 85g bag? Just 32 seconds. **watercressfestival.org**

RHS CHELSEA FLOWER SHOW

The world's most prestigious flower show brings together extraordinary show gardens and some of the best international nurseries and growers over five days at the Royal Hospital, Chelsea. Get expert advice, spot emerging trends, find out about the science behind horticulture and indulge in some garden-related retail therapy as you admire incredible horticultural creativity. **rhs.org.uk**

Chelsea's Floral Marquee

Pioneers: the world's first passenger jet stewardesses

70 YEARS OF PASSENGER JETS

On 2 May 1952, the de Havilland Comet 1 was introduced into BOAC's flight service, heralding a new age in passenger travel. It was the world's first pressurised commercial jet airliner – and the source of enormous national pride, setting new standards for both flight performance and passenger comfort. Large tables and windows gave an unaccustomed feeling of luxury, and the planes also included a galley serving hot and cold food and drinks, plus a bar and separate men's and women's toilets. The aircraft was an instant hit with the passengers, including Queen Elizabeth II, the Queen Mother and HRH Princess Margaret, who were all VIPs on a special flight in June 1953. In its first year, the Comets carried more than 30,000 passengers, with at least eight flights departing London each week, destined for Johannesburg, Tokyo, Singapore and Colombo.

GLYNDEBOURNE FESTIVAL

Top-notch opera in the heart of the Sussex countryside, the season begins in May. Formal dress is the norm, with audiences dressing up in their best finery and enjoying the 90-minute interval with a picnic in the gardens. **glyndebourne.com**

COOPERS HILL CHEESE ROLLING

What do you get when you combine the spring bank holiday, a very steep hill and a wheel of Double Gloucester? The answer is this world-famous, bizarre and really quite dangerous event, at Brockworth, Gloucestershire. The cheese reaches speeds of more than 70mph (and it's not unheard of for entrants to be hospitalised) but if you're the winner you get to keep it! Enter at your own risk. **facebook.com/cheeserolling/**

THE ELGAR FESTIVAL

This four-day musical celebration of our greatest composer, based in and around his home town of

Worcester, combines an ambitious programme of concerts, workshops and recitals with plays, exhibits, talks and community projects. It's held annually during the weekend closest to Elgar's birthday (2 June, 1857). **elgarfestival.org**

LICHFIELD BOWER

Dating back to 1145 and Henry II's demands for an annual muster of fighting men. Back then they were assembled before magistrates at a "bower house" decorated with laurel and lilac, given free beef and wine and then paraded around the city. These days, there's still a procession, plus fairground attractions, arts and crafts, food and market stalls, and live music. **lichfieldbower.co.uk**

BRIGHTON FESTIVALS

An array of festivals take place during May in and around Brighton. There's Brighton Festival itself, a three-week celebration of music, theatre, dance, circus, art, film and literature running since 1967; Brighton Fringe – anyone can take part, anything goes (!) – Artists Open Houses each weekend and The Great Escape, the festival for new music. At nearby stately home Charleston, its festival looks at art, literature, politics and ideas past and present, with an eye to challenging the status quo. **visitbrighton.com**

BATH FESTIVAL

Bath's flagship festival of music and literature brings world-class artists and authors to the Georgian city and is accompanied by a Fringe Festival covering myriad art forms. It all ends with a Finale Weekend that's an extravaganza of music, food and fun. **bathfestivals.org.uk**

TORTOISE FAIR

A summer afternoon of tortoise racing is now a firm fixture in the Oxford year. Starting as a gentlemanly challenge issued by Oxford's Corpus Christi College students to their counterparts in Oriel, it's usually held on the sixth Sunday of the Trinity term. Live music, entertainment and refreshments accompany the main reptilian race. **corpusjcr.org/clubs-and-societies/tortoise-fair**

DECORATIVE LIVING FAIR

The much-loved Decorative Living Fair at Eridge Park, a country estate on the borders of Kent and Sussex, has been run since 2006, bringing together a wide variety of dealers in antique, vintage and contemporary decorative goods. The fair has a dedicated following and a relaxed, convivial atmosphere. **decorativelivingfair.co.uk**

BRISTOL WALK FEST

Get walking in and around the city of Bristol, with heritage tours, nature walks, explorations of street art, wild food forays, walking sports tasters and woodland story times. **bristolwalkfest.com**

CRAB & LOBSTER FESTIVAL

Cromer and Sheringham get together to enjoy food, art and music in this lively celebration of their seafaring heritage and Norfolk fishing communities. The event takes place on 15 and 16 May this year, starting off with a variety concert, and featuring heritage demonstrations, a cookery theatre, the "Boatiful" Boat Art Trail and plenty more to entertain.
facebook.com/CrabandLobsterFestival

Morris dancers in Sheringham for the fishy festival

MAY DANCING

Dancing is strongly associated with this month, with Morris groups and maypole dancing. There's also the Jack in the Green, a man encased in a tall framework of foliage and flowers. The Knutsford Jack is probably the oldest, but there are around 20 up and down the country, including Deptford in London, Bristol, Hastings and Whitstable. Another character that can sometimes be seen "dancing" through towns on May Day or as part of a festival is the Hobby Horse, which performs antics with a folk band as part of a tradition dating back to the 18th century. The Minehead Hobby Horse takes to the streets on the first three days of the month, while in Padstow there are two 'Obby Osses which parade around the town. Lastly, an intriguing dance takes place in Helston, Cornwall, as part of its annual Flora Day (this year on Saturday, 7 May).
themorrisring.org; padstowobbyoss.wordpress.com; helstonfloraday.org.uk

The Knutsford Jack dressed as a tree in 1976

>

JUNE 2022

ISLE OF WIGHT FESTIVAL

The UK summer festival calendar is traditionally kicked off in the Isle of Wight with a diverse line-up that showcases new and emerging talent as well as legendary names in the music world. Organisers take pride in offering performances that you might not see elsewhere, as well as a uniquely relaxed atmosphere and friendly vibe. **isleofwightfestival.com**

Crowds on the Isle of Wight

THE CHAMPIONSHIPS, WIMBLEDON

Our favourite tennis tournament started in 1877 with 22 amateur tennis players who answered an ad in the leisure magazine *The Field*. These days, the attendance is more than 500,000, with a TV audience of millions around the globe and prize money totalling almost £40m. This year's tournament takes place from 27 June to 10 July. See our feature, p44. **wimbledon.com**

ROYAL ASCOT

Very much loved by Her Majesty the Queen, Royal Ascot attracts many of the world's finest horses, which compete for more than £8m in prize money. It is also world-famous for its sartorial splendour and magnificent millinery. Don't miss the Royal Procession each day at 2pm sharp: the Landau carriages, led by four Windsor greys, approach along the famous Straight Mile, signalling the start of the Royal Meeting. **ascot.co.uk**

Romping home at Royal Ascot

EPSOM DERBY

The Derby is a flat horse race run over a mile and a half and open to three-year-old colts and fillies. Alongside the racing, expect lots of people dressed up to the nines, plenty of picnics, live music and all sorts of other entertainment, from skydivers to celebrity DJ parties. **thejockeyclub.co.uk**

TROOPING THE COLOUR

Trooping the Colour – a royal inspection of troops – has marked the official birthday of the British Sovereign for more than 260 years. The display of military precision, horsemanship and fanfare moves from Buckingham Palace to Horse Guards Parade, and concludes with an RAF fly-past and gun salute from Green Park. **qbp.army.mod.uk**

WOOLFEST

This celebration of natural fibres – from fleece and livestock to yarn and finished craft – features more or less anything wool-related that you can think of, including a mass knit-in, at Cockermouth in Cumbria. **woolfest.co.uk**

THE GREAT KNARESBOROUGH BED RACE

About 90 teams race to raise money for local Yorkshire charities along a gruelling 2.4 mile course that includes steep slopes, cobbles and an icy swim at the end. The twist? They're all pushing a wheeled "bed" and a passenger. As well as the time trial, there's also a splendid fancy-dress procession, with prizes for the best-dressed teams. **bedrace.co.uk**

GOLOWAN

Cornish towns and villages once honoured midsummer with bonfires, flaming tar barrels and burning torches – until the late 19th century, when the perceived fire risk made insurance premiums too expensive. In 1991, however, the town of Penzance revived the tradition with a day of celebration. The event has now grown into a ten-day community-led extravaganza, with a serpent dance, Mock Mayor

CRAFT FESTIVAL

One of the most important fairs on the craft calendar, hundreds of designer-maker stands, hand-picked for absolute top quality, are the heart of this annual three-day festival in Bovey Tracey, Devon, while alongside are workshops and demonstrations, live music and locally sourced food. **craftfestival.co.uk**

Craft Festival at Bovey Tracey

Chester's Watch Parade was first held in 1498

MIDSUMMER WATCH PARADE

One of the oldest festivals in Britain, Chester's colourful parade was first held in 1498. While many Tudor pageants featured enormous "giants", Chester was unique in parading a whole family of them: mother, father and two daughters. They were accompanied by other huge, fantastic beasts and enormous moving floats called the "Mounts". Announced by a loudly beating drum, it must have been the most exciting event of the year. However, Puritanism triumphed over pageantry in the 1660s, and the parade lapsed until the late 20th century, when it was revived with a single giant in 1989. The parade has since grown bigger every year: these days schools and youth groups spend weeks creating characters, and it is a highlight of the Cheshire calendar. **midsummerwatch.co.uk**

election, quayside fair, workshops, talks and a fireworks display. On Mazey Day, the final Saturday, a series of colourful parades are watched by tens of thousands of locals and visitors, and the whole town becomes a huge market place for the day, with traders selling all manner of goods as well as food from around the world. **golowanfestival.org**

FIRST LIGHT FESTIVAL

Enjoy the longest day at the place where the sun rises first – Lowestoft. This relatively new festival started in 2019 and has been postponed for two years to make its return in 2022. There's music, food and fun and it's all held on the beach. **firstlightlowestoft.com**

SUMMER SOLSTICE

The summer solstice is one of the rare occasions when members of the public are allowed to enter the stone circle at Stonehenge. The sarsen stones, erected in the centre of the site in about 2,500 BC, were carefully positioned to line up with the movements of the sun, and at sunrise on 21 June its first rays shine from behind the Heel Stone. Thousands of people gather from all over the world to witness the spectacle, and English Heritage provides free managed open access for individuals and groups conducting their own forms of ceremony and celebration. No alcohol is allowed at this peaceful, positive event – but if you wish to bring ceremonial mead you should contact customer services. **www.english-heritage.org.uk/visit/places/stonehenge**

THE ART AND ANTIQUES FAIR

This is the capital's longest-running and most-respected vetted art and antiques fair and attracts enthusiasts from across the world to Olympia looking for that inspirational, unique piece. **olympia-art-antiques.com**

The Art and Antiques Fair at London's Olympia

WYBUNBURY FIG PIE WAKES

Every year, on a Saturday in June, the local community in Wybunbury, Cheshire, bakes fig pies and competes to roll them down the hill outside the Swan Inn. It dates back to at least the early 1800s, though there was a break in the 20th century due to "unruly brawling". Revived in 1995 to raise money for the village's church tower, it's now a charming and popular event, with stalls, refreshments, and entertainment. This year it takes place on 11 June. **facebook.com/wybunburyfigpie**

ROYAL ACADEMY SUMMER EXHIBITION

Anyone can enter their works of art into the Royal Academy's summer exhibition, which features new and recent art created by everyone from emerging artists to the biggest names in contemporary art and architecture. Many of the galleries in Burlington House in London's Piccadilly are hung densely, high and low. While some are dedicated to a single artist, others will feature film, photography or installations. **royalacademy.org.uk**

The Royal Academy Summer Exhibition

Images: Shutterstock and Alamy

ENGLISH BRIDGES

CLIFTON, BRISTOL

Mairi Hughes delves into the history of the Clifton Suspension Bridge

Brunel's SS Great Britain

Lion cubs at Bristol Zoo

BBC Bristol Broadcasting House

FROM its popular zoo to its picturesque harbour to its variety of museums and galleries, there is much to see and do on a visit to Bristol. It is, however, a small patch of pavement in the Clifton area where more photographs are taken than any other part of the city, according to Google. The three-yard-square area provides prime views of the distinctive sweeping chain cradling the 700 feet of the Clifton Suspension Bridge, standing 246 feet above the Avon Gorge.

Completed in 1864, this Grade I listed bridge was both the highest and longest bridge in the world at the time of its construction. The bridge's spectacular views of the River Avon, from both from its footpath and the road joining North Somerset's Leigh Woods and Bristol's Clifton, ensure its acclaimed reputation.

Despite the popularity of the bridge, it almost never came to be. When 24-year-old Isambard Kingdom Brunel won a competition which allowed him to design the Clifton Suspension Bridge, it was set to be his first major commission. Brunel's plans to stray from the 19th-century norm of wooden bridges in favour of iron and suspension were revolutionary. However, after construction of the bridge got underway, it ran into financial difficulties which forced the project to be abandoned in 1843. For many years, the bridge's towers stood isolated on either side of the Avon Gorge.

Brunel went on to become an engineering giant and subsequently worked on several projects across the country, including acting as chief engineer to the Great Western Railway. However, the Clifton Suspension Bridge, which he described as "my first child, my darling", remained unfinished. It was not until after Brunel's death, when engineer John Halkshaw was dismantling Brunel's Hungerford Bridge in London, that it was realised the links from this bridge could be used to complete the Clifton Suspension Bridge.

And so Halkshaw, teamed up with William Henry Barlow, finally finished the Clifton Suspension Bridge as a tribute to Brunel, five years after his death and 33 years after construction had begun.

The Clifton Suspension Bridge is now one of the oldest surviving suspension bridges in the world. Brunel's design has proved sturdy enough to see over 150 years of traffic, and the Institution of Civil Engineers estimate that around 97 per cent of the iron work on the bridge today is original. While it was built primarily for horse-drawn traffic, it now provides a passage for 11,000 cars every day, and has a pathway on either side for pedestrians. The bridge is a popular vantage point during Bristol's International Balloon Fiesta, when it provides the perfect spot to watch the ascent of hundreds of hot air balloons.

Visitors to the bridge can stop off at the Visitor Centre in Leigh Woods, the Clifton Observatory in Clifton, take a guided tour, or simply walk over themselves. Find out more at cliftonbridge.org.uk.

THINGS TO DO IN BRISTOL

Brunel's *SS Great Britain*

If you're eager to find out more about Isambard Kingdom Brunel, be sure to stop off at Brunel's *SS Great Britain*. Discover what was in its day the world's longest passenger ship. Admission includes entry to "Being Brunel", exploring the life and legacy of the trailblazing engineer. **Gas Ferry Rd, Great Western Dockyard, Bristol BS1 6TY. 0117 926 0680; ssgreatbritain.org**

Bristol Zoo

Catch this much-loved zoo at its historic current site before it moves out of town at the end of 2022. The zoo is also a conservation and education charity and strives to maintain biodiversity through breeding endangered species. Enjoy the animals and learn about its mission to help the natural world. **College Rd, Clifton, Bristol BS8 3HA. 0117 428 5300; bristolzoo.org.uk**

BBC Bristol

Go behind the scenes on a tour of BBC Bristol. Tours give an insight into programmes made in the studios, including *Antiques Roadshow*, *Countryfile*, *Poetry Please* and *Blue Planet II*. Try your hand at reading the news and star in your very own radio drama. **Broadcasting House, 31-33 Whiteladies Rd, Bristol BS8 2LR. 0117 973 2211; bbc.co.uk/showsandtours/tours/bbc-bristol**

Images: Alamy, Shutterstock

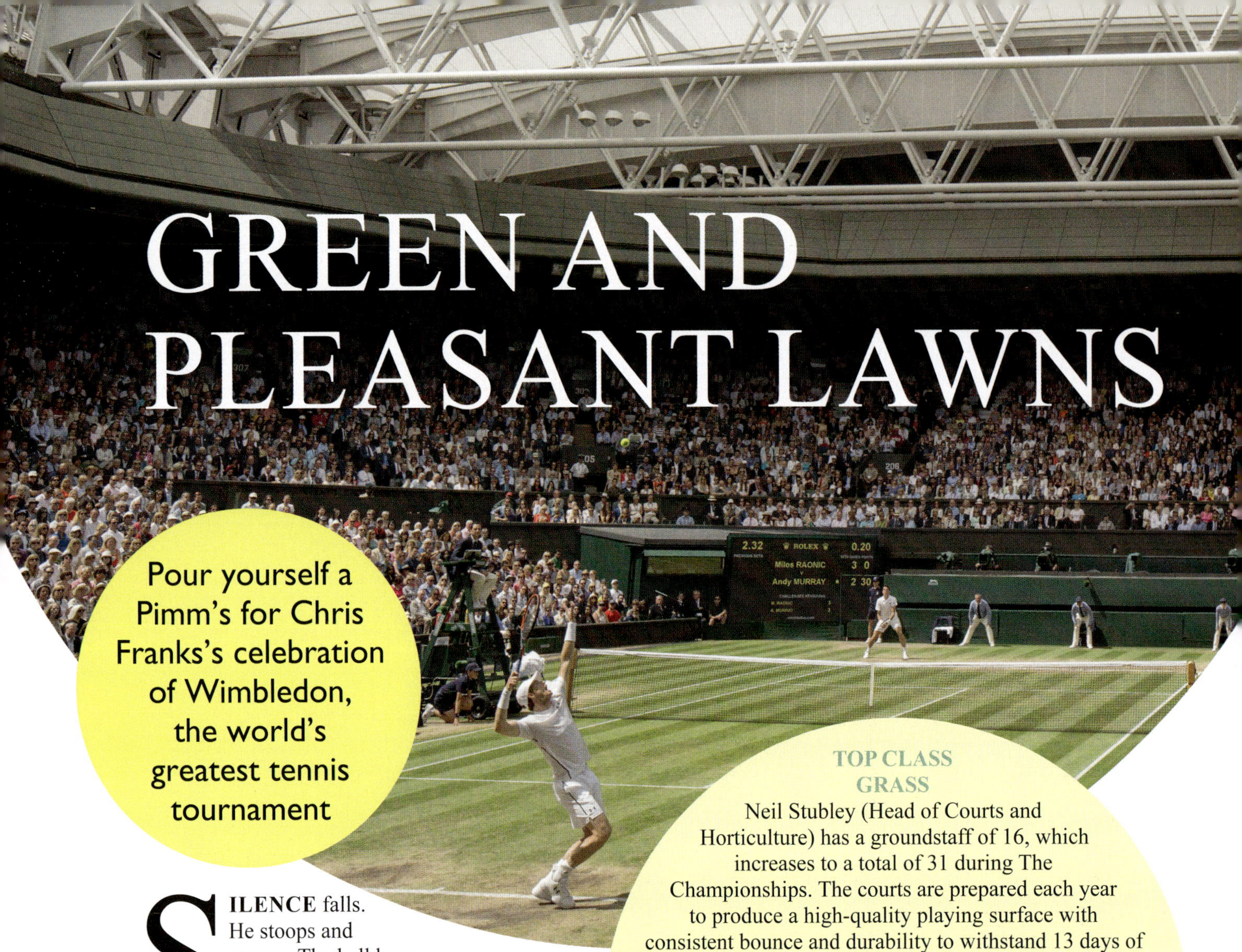

GREEN AND PLEASANT LAWNS

Pour yourself a Pimm's for Chris Franks's celebration of Wimbledon, the world's greatest tennis tournament

SILENCE falls. He stoops and pauses. The ball hops between the sallow grass and his deftly flicking wrist. Dup, dup, dup . . .

Slowly, he raises his head, his eyes passing over the opponent across the net, then lifting ever skywards until fixed on the zenith. His left arm extends, his fingers unfurl and like a bird taking flight, the yellow ball springs free. It slows and hovers. His eye locks. And all the time his spine arching, his right arm cocking, the racquet head coiling like a cobra to strike. Everything freezes . . .

AELTC/Thomas Lovelock

Preparing those make-or-break lines . . .

He leaps. His arm detonates. The racquet lashes like a whip. Thock! The bird is now a bullet, zipping at 130 miles per hour.

This is Wimbledon, the most famous tennis tournament in the world. Hearing the name conjures a whirlwind of images. There are lots of tennis tournaments, but none has the magic of Wimbledon and it's not obvious why this is.

Wimbledon certainly has a long and rich history. The oldest of the four Grand Slam events, the first tournament was held in 1877, when 22 men competed with snowshoe racquets and hand-sewn balls in front of 200 people. It took Spencer Gore 48 minutes to beat W.C. Marshall and claim the first men's title. The first women's competition took place seven years

TOP CLASS GRASS

Neil Stubley (Head of Courts and Horticulture) has a groundstaff of 16, which increases to a total of 31 during The Championships. The courts are prepared each year to produce a high-quality playing surface with consistent bounce and durability to withstand 13 days of attrition from competitors. Following each Championship, renovation of Centre Court and No.1 Court is undertaken – the only two courts put in abeyance after The Championships conclude. Once the grass court season ends in September, the rest of the courts undergo renovation. They are scarified, top dressed, levelled and additional seeding sown. Rye grass is used throughout and a thin top dressing comprising sand or a prepared soil mix is applied thinly to the surface of the lawn. This is followed by winter feeding and regular cutting in spring. During The Championships, daily mowing, rolling and re-lining takes place.

later. Britain's most successful champions come from these early years, with William Renshaw winning seven times and Charlotte "Lottie" Dodd five. Aged just fifteen, Lottie Dodd is still the youngest woman ever to win the ladies' singles.

Wimbledon grew in popularity through the first half of the 20th century, but it was in 1968 that the pace of change accelerated. That was the first year of the Open era, when professionals were allowed to take part. Until then, the tournament had been for amateurs only, but the situation was nonsensical. Wimbledon, supposedly a top event, was barring the world's top players. In an all-Australian men's final, Rod Laver beat Tony Roche to earn £2,000, while Billie Jean King took the women's title, earning £750.

With prize money now at stake, players looked to gain every advantage. There were experiments in racquet technology with steel, aluminium and composite materials, but the substance that was to revolutionise Wimbledon was graphite. A type of carbon, graphite, in its purest form, is lighter than paper and stronger than steel. Racquets became lighter and stronger, and with vibration dampened and twisting minimised, strokes were much more accurate. There had always been big hitters at Wimbledon. Now they were no longer armed with blunderbusses but sniper rifles. Graphite racquets first gained popularity in the 1970s, with the last wooden racquet used at the tournament in 1987.

Greater speeds and finer placement of the ball meant that the human eye couldn't keep up, though. Arguments between line judges and players began to mar the tournament, none more so than three times winner John McEnroe's notorious outburst in 1981. His yell of "You cannot be serious" is part of tennis legend and became the title of his 2002 autobiography.

So how fast were those sniper bullets? Through the Eighties and Nineties, Pete Sampras and Goran Ivanisevic were dominating Wimbledon with serves regularly exceeding 125 mph. But with points over so quickly, the men's tournament began to be seen as boring. In the 1994 Sampras-Ivanisevic final, around a fifth of the points were aces and only one rally went beyond four strokes. To preserve Wimbledon's reputation, The All England Lawn Tennis Club made changes to the ball, reducing the air pressure and increasing the length of its fluffy surface, or nap, to slow it down.

Longer rallies resumed but the problem of close line calls became more acute. Cyclops, the infrared line monitoring system used in the 1980s, helped on the serve, but >

BLOOMING LOVELY

Capturing the ambience of a traditional country garden at the 42-acre site is the task of Head Gardener Martyn Falconer and his dedicated team of seven full-time gardeners. Another 10 additional gardeners are drafted in from April to September. There'll be over 50,000 plants at the garden's annual peak: some 200 hanging baskets, 15,000 window and floral borders, a mile of beech, holly and yew hedges, a rose arbour and masonry walls, such as the 64-foot ivy-clad Centre Court wall, all requiring attention. Plant colours are selected to reflect the Wimbledon logo, with purple, mauves, whites and greens, including *Hebe* 'Caledonia', *Liriope* 'Big Blue,'(for purples) and *Bergenia* 'Bressingham White', *Euonymus fortunei* 'Emerald Gaiety' and *Polypodium vulgare* (for white/green). Alliums, foxgloves, roses, petunias, hydrangeas, lupins and alchemilla are also abundant.

Federer salutes the crowd as runner-up, 2019

AELTC/Ian Walton

There are 50,000 plants to tend during The Championships

Wimbledon's patron, the Duchess of Cambridge, greeting ball boys and girls

> wasn't always reliable, and a solution covering the entire court was needed. Cue Hawk-Eye, introduced in 2007. It works by positioning 10 cameras round the court and taking 60 images per second. Computers triangulate the 3D location of the ball and extrapolate a trajectory to work out the exact position at the point of bounce.

Players have mixed views about it. After a Hawk-Eye decision went his way by just one millimetre in 2015, two times winner Andy Murray said:

"I think Hawk-Eye's great. I've been playing under Hawk-Eye for 10 years now . . . That was a very important one today."

Others are less convinced.

"What I struggle with is, I don't think it's 100 per cent accurate," says eight times champion, Roger Federer. "Let's say 99 per cent, fine. It's still not 100 per cent . . . I still see calls I don't understand."

With just a 2.2 millimetre margin of error, Hawk-Eye has certainly obviated disputes between players and line judges, though it shouldn't be confused with Wimbledon's real hawk, whose job it is to patrol the courts and scare away pigeons. His name is Rufus.

The slower ball didn't dissuade the big servers, though. The fastest men's serve at Wimbledon was delivered by Taylor Dent in 2010 at 148 mph, with Venus Williams setting the women's record at 129 mph in 2008. The speed is measured as the ball leaves the racquet, but with it now slowing by two thirds once it reaches the opposite baseline, a different weapon began to dominate Wimbledon: the return.

For the last 17 years, the men's singles has been won by just four players: Federer, Nadal, Murray and Djokovic. While none is a huge server, all are master returners. In his 2016 final against Milos Raonic, Murray faced the fastest serve of the tournament that year, at a scorching 147 mph. Not only did he return it, he won the point. Opinion on Djokovic is divided. Some say he is the greatest returner of serve today, some say of all time.

Developments at Wimbledon have gone beyond the court, though. Since 1922 only eight championships have passed without rain delays, prompting the installation of retractable roofs: the first on Centre Court in 2009 and another on No.1 Court in 2019.

HELPING HANDS

More than 6,000 additional staff are employed in the lead up to and during Wimbledon, including Service Stewards from the Armed Forces and London Fire Brigade. For the Ball Boys and Girls (BBGs) it's an intensive training process. More than 700 apply from local schools, but only 250 will make the cut after demonstrating a wide understanding of tennis. During the court practices they need to be fast, alert, self-confident and adaptable to situations.

AELTC/Ian Walton

Updating the board with the day's matches

Murray realising his lifelong dream, 2013. He was Britain's first male champ for 77 years

Each roof takes 10 minutes to deploy and weighs 3,000 tonnes. Yet, for all the technological advancement, Wimbledon retains some of its oldest traditions. It's the only major tournament where the dress code for players is still almost entirely white, a rule dating back to Victorian times when propriety was offended by sweat patches on coloured clothing. It is also the only major tournament played on the sport's original surface of grass, and the only one that has never changed location.

Much of the tournament's appeal is in the intensity of the battle. There is something primordial about a one-on-one duel and Wimbledon has seen many great finals over the decades. In a sense, every one is a classic, pitting two top-class athletes against each other. Every final has moments of brilliance, with joy, despair and everything in between. Some have been truly memorable. Like 1975, when Arthur Ashe became the first black man ever to win. Or 1977, when Virginia Wade was the last British woman to win. Then 1980 and 1981, the Borg and McEnroe years, the most famous personality clash in tennis history: the calm measured Borg and the brash outspoken McEnroe, for many the greatest Wimbledon rivalry ever.

Wade, our last woman to win in 1977

In 1985, the year of youth, Boris Becker became the youngest man to win, aged just 17. 1990 was the record year, with the ninth victory of Martina Navratilova, the most singles titles ever. Then came 2001, the fairy-tale year, when Goran Ivanisevic, twice-defeated finalist and on the verge of retirement, was offered a wild card to compete. Against all the odds, he became the only man to win on a wild card entry. And, of course, 2013, the history year, with Andy Murray the first British man in 77 years to lift the trophy.

ALL IN THE PLANNING

Wimbledon is managed by The All England Lawn Tennis Club (AELTC) who oversee, plan and execute this massive global event. For Matthew Crawcour, (Head of Championships Operations), planning starts very early on. Even before the conclusion of the current Championships, Matthew and up to 40 teams and groups are hard at work assessing the success of the tournament. "The numbers are always very favourable in terms of feedback from our guests, but we are always looking to improve upon them and move the dial to the highest level," Matthew says. "It's incredibly important to us that we respect our heritage and traditions . . . People come to Wimbledon for more than a sporting event and the challenge is always for the team to ensure a memorable guest experience that reflects the ethos of tennis in an English garden."

Wimbledon isn't just about tennis. Throughout The Championships in 2019 it employed around 6,000 people, over half of them caterers, serving up 18,000 portions of fish and chips, 192,000 portions of strawberries and 276,000 glasses of Pimm's. It is the largest annual sport catering operation in Europe.

It is also a great fund-raiser, with ticket resales and other donations contributing over £384,000 to charity. In addition to the 500,000 visitors through the door, it is watched on TV by millions.

Wimbledon is an occasion, a celebration, and there is something quintessentially English about it, with people in white playing games on green and pleasant lawns. It has the feel-good factor and epitomises that much-loved, yet so rarely seen thing, the fine British summer.

The real magic of Wimbledon is that it's the dream. While other tournaments are prestigious, the one the players dream of winning is Wimbledon. Take the words of three times champion, Billie Jean King: "Everything was about Wimbledon when I was growing up." Five times champion, Bjorn Borg said: "Wimbledon always meant something special to me. It's always been a tournament that every player in the world has a dream about."

Or, five times winner, Novak Djokovic: "To be part of this tournament and eventually one day get a chance to win it . . . It was something I always dreamed of."

Or, the greatest Wimbledonian on singles titles, Martina Navratilova. Referring to a piece of grass she plucked from Centre Court after losing her last singles final, she said: "I have so many memories, but picking out the blade of grass, that's what people seem to remember. I still have that blade of grass."

Wimbledon is the one that ignited their passion, that inspired them to pick up a racquet. It's their life's mission, galvanising them to new heights, and when they step out on Centre Court, you sense it: the steely concentration in their faces, the joy and agony in their cries. With each sinew-splitting scramble for the ball, you feel their desperation, as if every point is life or death. For them, it is.

This passion reaches a climax at championship point and as that bullet ricochets off the line for a clean winner, the dream is made reality. Game, set, match – and the tournament. The cheers erupt. And just for a moment, we all feel like champions.

Wimbledon 2022, 27 June to 10 July; wimbledon.com

Box copy: John Greeves; Images: Shutterstock, Alamy unless stated otherwise

70 Glorious Years

As the nation prepares for a four-day Jubilee Weekend at the start of June, our photo-essay looks at HM The Queen's 70-year reign

Arriving in UK as sovereign, 1952

IT'S an extraordinary reign, from the moment a poised young Queen stepped down from an aircraft on to British soil for the first time as monarch. It has been a reign marked by dignity, duty and stability that has earned the affection and respect of her subjects across the UK and the Commonwealth.

Our pictures show 70 years of HM Queen Elizabeth II, and its a reign which has seen extraordinary technological, scientific and social change. The pictures tell the story of her role as sovereign, but also as a mother of a family that has been constantly in the public eye. She is the UK's longest-reigning monarch, and has met some 14 Prime Ministers, from Winston Churchill to Boris Johnson.

She has been there in times of triumph and has supported the nation in times of disaster. Her role has taken her all over the world and her face is said to be the most reproduced image of any human being since Jesus Christ.

Royal Family at Buckingham Palace after the Coronation, 1953

At Balmoral in 1960 with Princess Anne and Prince Andrew

Above: With Chancellor Kohl, Ronald Reagan and Margaret Thatcher, 1984
Right: On a visit to Thailand in 1972

At Royal Ascot, a diary date kept every year, June 2010

With Barack and Michelle Obama on a state visit to England, 2011

A family portrait at Buckingham Palace in 1972 on the Queen and Prince Philip's silver wedding anniversary

Images: Shutterstock

On the balcony at the Trooping of the Colour in June 2015

At the annual Easter service in 2019

MEET THE JET SET

Linda Barrett on the superstars of the RAF – the Red Arrows!

Soaring across the South Devon coastline . . .

DOZING on Blackpool beach on a hot summer's day in 1970, I was abruptly jolted back to reality by a tremendous roaring of engines directly above me. It was my first encounter with the Red Arrows. I had neither seen nor heard of them before, but from that day I was totally hooked. Their skill and daring as aerobatic pilots still never ceases to take my breath away.

The Red Arrows are the public face of the RAF and have a number of roles, with one of the most important being "to inspire". Many people join the RAF having seen and been influenced by them as children; I myself spent three-and-a-half very memorable years in the WRAF, working in Personnel and Administration, before leaving upon marriage.

The Royal Air Force Aerobatic Team, the Red Arrows, formed in 1964 when the RAF merged its existing display teams, including the Black Arrows, from whom they took their name. The RAF wanted to showcase their elite pilots and cutting-edge technology to the British public here and beyond these shores, and they quickly achieved iconic status. Red was chosen as a tribute to the Red Pelicans, another early RAF display team.

Recruitment into the team is tough. Before they can even apply, pilots must complete at least 1,500 hours' flying and be graded as an above average pilot. They must have also completed at least one front-line operational tour. Those who make it on to the shortlist face a week of gruelling tests and assessments. As well as a flying test, they are graded on how they handle media activity. They also have a formal interview and, most importantly, pass peer assessments. Approximately 30 people apply each year for two or three available slots, and those who make it are the crème de la crème of RAF pilots.

Rehearsing moves over RAF Scampton

The team of nine jets is split into two sections. The front five aircraft are known as Enid, named after children's author Enid Blyton and her *Famous Five* series. New team members will normally fly in this section under the watchful eye of Red 1. More experienced pilots will move back in the formation. The rear four aircraft are referred to as Gypo, named after a former boss from the 1960s. It is the pilots in Gypo, Reds 6 to 9, who perform the more dynamic and complicated manoeuvres.

Flying in formation is challenging. The concentration required by each of the pilots, with a constant awareness of the aircraft around them, their position within the formation and a focus on the team leader, is so intense that it is all consuming. The team members take their instructions from Red 1, who speaks to them over the radio in a staccato voice. For example, he may say "Pull-ing-up-now!" and everyone in the team will move as one on the "N" of the "now". A great deal of training goes on during winter, especially for new pilots, ahead of the summer airshows.

"On a typical winter training >

Blue skies for the show at Hastings . . .

> day, we will gather in work at 08.15 hours," says Squadron Leader Jon Bond (Bondy). "We look at the daily weather forecast and discuss the day's training schedule. Initially the training is split between Enid and Gypo, but as we get towards February/March both formations will start training and integrating together.

"We aim to fly three times a day, five days a week, if weather and aircraft serviceability allows. During our pre-sortie briefing we will talk through all of the planned manoeuvres, including potential emergencies we could face carrying out that particular serial.

"We then get changed into our flying kit. We wear special trousers which counteract the G-force that the manoeuvres induce and stop us from effectively blacking out. Gypo could be pulling up to seven times their own body weight in "positive G." Their flying kit is very important. If the blood pools in the lower half of the body they can lose consciousness. The trousers they wear are very tight fitting. When pressurised they press firmly on the pilot's abdomen and legs and stop the blood draining away from the brain.

"If all goes to plan we would finish work at around 16.30 hours after thoroughly debriefing all of our three sorties in turn," Bondy continues. "The debrief is arguably the most important part of the sortie cycle for us. We aim to highlight any errors from an almost real-time video replay and correct these on our next flight.

"The team places safety as its highest priority and there are escape manoeuvres for each formation, allowing the pilot to take his aircraft safely away from the rest of the formation should they ever need to do so."

The Synchro Pair (Reds 6 and 7) perform some of the most popular manoeuvres such as "low head on pass", where the two aircraft fly towards each other at great speed, only separating at the last moment.

Bondy was Red 6 and leader of the Synchro Pair in 2021. "Synchro are the two aircraft that perform the low and fast opposing passes that you see in the second half of the show, and can have closing speeds towards each other of over 800 mph whilst being laterally only 100 feet apart. It takes very specific training for this role, as it is both physically and mentally demanding, but it is, ultimately, incredibly rewarding."

Bringing the jet to a stop

With intense skill training and team building done in the winter, summer is the time for practising the display in between shows. The display sequence is decided in winter, ultimately gaining approval to perform in the coming season once Public Display Authority is granted, following thorough scrutiny by the team's Air Officer Commanding – a very senior RAF officer. Once achieved, the pilots are allowed to swap their regular green flying suits for their iconic red ones, and their support team will don blue – hence their nickname The Blues.

From engineers and technicians to photographers, from logistics staff to drivers, it takes around 100 support workers to keep the Red Arrows flying. At the start of every season 10 people (usually nine engineers and a photographer) will be chosen from the Blues to fly with the pilots to and from airshows to keep the jets in perfect nick and be on hand in case of any technical problems. These 10 are known as Circus. Flying in the back seat, they take their call sign from the pilot with which they fly. The Circus member who flies with Red 3 will take the call sign Circus 3.

Corporal Lydia Ford is an avionics technician who joined the Blues in 2017 and looks after the instruments on the aircraft. She was a member of Circus in 2018 and 2019. In 2019 she flew with Squadron Leader Bond, who was then Red 7.

"It was an amazing experience which will stay with me for the rest of my life.

"The first few times pulling G can be quite tiring and some people are physically sick, but just like training your body on a treadmill, you do get used to it. It's the same with flying upside down: people respond differently initially,

SHOOTING THE SKIES

Robyn Ferris has been passionate about photography for as long as she can remember. She was given a Kodak Instamatic when she was 10 and was instantly fascinated by being able to freeze memories forever. The kit has moved on since then, but the fascination remains and Robyn has become an amateur photographer with a difference.

Summer weekends see her pack her Canon 7DMK2 and lenses to head for the airshows. She's a self-confessed airshow fanatic and a huge fan of The Red Arrows. On average she clocks up 15-20 airshows a year travelling from her home in the South East to events far and wide, and has travelled as far away as Stornoway and all across Ireland to follow her passion.

Robyn began going to airshows religiously from 1999, with her now husband, Ben.

"Initially, it was just the odd show and generally the free ones like Eastbourne, Dartmouth and Southend. Ben wasn't particularly enthused, but I got hooked. In 2014, I attended over 20 Red Arrows displays. I remember Martin Pert, former team leader, saying that he reckoned I'd been to more displays that year than anyone not on the team."

The social side of things is at least as important as the photography and events to Robyn. Many friends she's made are members of the Red Arrows' support team, The Blues. "I've made many good friends over the years and that means a lot to me. I'm also proud of the 'Circus at Work' project that I did. I started it in 2014 and it ran for a couple of years. Until I did that pretty much no-one gave a thought to what they do. I'm pleased to have played a part in getting them more noticed.

"I'd got to know Ross Harrison via Twitter. At the time he was Circus 8. I took some shots of Ross and the other guys at Biggin Hill. This was in the June and the photos went down a storm. A couple of weeks later he arranged for me to go airside at Bristol Airport so I could take more shots of the Circus guys at work, and again the photos were a great success."

Robyn's photographic skills have earned her many followers on social media. She has over 15,000 on Instagram alone, many from the who's who of aviation. The Red Arrows and The Typhoon Display Team, as well as individual Reds and Blues, past and present, are some of the people to follow her.

Robyn is modest about it all. "I really appreciate everyone who follows me. I don't see those followers as being any more important than anyone else." Humble though she is, and for someone who has never had any formal training, there are many who admire her skills behind a camera. As for the future, Robyn doesn't show signs of giving up on the airshow scene any time soon. "I have my favourites places which I'd love to go back to. Jersey and Portrush, for example. I find airshows tremendous fun, and as long as that continues so will I."

but everyone gets used to it.

"Bondy let me pull some G force once and the aircraft just responded, no shaking or anything like that, though when they do certain manoeuvres, like the Spaghetti Break, and have to pull the air brake out, the aircraft does shake a bit.

"The Hawk has a maximum speed of 645 mph. but you don't feel how fast you're travelling; it's just like being on a commercial jet, but you see it at low level when you see the houses and traffic whizzing by. It's incredible."

The Reds act as ambassadors for the UK both at home and abroad, and in their time they have performed over 4,900 displays in 57 countries. In 2018, the RAF's centenary year, the team spearheaded events to both celebrate and inspire. Those of us who saw the fly-past over The Mall in June of that year were reminded just how loved they are. We witnessed an amazing and emotional display of skilful airmanship throughout the RAF in everything from Spitfires, Hurricanes and a Lancaster, but as soon as the Red Arrows came into view the loudest of cheers went up from the crowd.

In 2019, the Red Arrows embarked on their largest-ever tour of the USA and Canada, supporting a range of UK interests from defence and trade to education and tourism across 11 weeks. There were 21 displays and 30 stunning flypasts completed over major landmarks and locations, including a baseball stadium in Washington DC and a mixed formation with the Canadian Forces' Snowbirds team over Toronto. An innovative marketing and media campaign made it the Red Arrows' most visible overseas activity yet, with almost two billion people reached.

Speaking after the Red Arrows returned to the UK, Antony Phillipson, HM Trade Commissioner for North America and British Consul-General in New York, said: "Their being here provided invaluable support to the >

Squadron Leader Jon Bond with Corporal Lydia Ford

> work of Her Majesty's Government in North America, whether connecting UK exporters with potential buyers, engaging current and potential investors to the UK or helping to build transatlantic partnerships across STEM fields – a priority for all three countries. The Reds, and the Blues, demonstrated once again that they are awesome ambassadors for the UK and showcased all that is great about Britain."

Honour, privilege and pride are words that come up again and again when speaking to Red Arrows pilots. Their level of pride in what they do is immense. "It is an absolute privilege to be part of the team. My years in the Red Arrows have been ones I will never forget," Bondy tells me.

Squadron Leader Tom Bould of Red 1 and the current team leader feels the same: "It is an absolute honour to lead The Red Arrows, showcasing, across the UK and overseas, a world-leading aerobatic display – representing the best of British. Months of hard work and preparation by pilots and support personnel go into a Red Arrows performance that will both uphold and build upon the distinguished history and legacy of our predecessors."

Of course, the pilots don't have an opportunity to see the crowd when they are flying, but they do enjoy meeting fans before or after shows and interacting with them on social media. Red 1 is no exception.

"Looping or rolling all nine aircraft together in a tight formation takes enormous concentration, but to see people's images of the show, often posted online, or to meet them in person at an event is even more humbling."

The last two years were as frustrating for the Red Arrows as they were for the rest of us. With all airshows cancelled in 2020, as well as many events in 2021, the team is eager to display a full season. "This year we look forward to displaying in all corners of the UK and seeing you in person both in the air and on the ground. Further afield we will continue to collaborate with strategic partners to promote a global Britain and fly the UK flag in the most colourful and dynamic way possible," Wing Commander David Montenegro, Officer Commanding The Red Arrows, tells me.

My heart soars. After a break, the joy of seeing The Red Arrows charging overhead once more might just be greater than ever.

EIGHT GREAT AIRSHOWS

Seafront displays are particularly popular

The Royal International Air Tattoo held each July at RAF Fairford, Gloucestershire, is the biggest military airshow in the world and supports the RAF Charitable Trust. It attracts over 150,000 visitors a year and participants from 25 countries. As well as an eight-and-a-half hour flying display, there's an RAF Experience and Vintage Village to enjoy.

Imperial War Museum at Duxford, Cambridge, has three airshows a year in May, July and September. Step back in time with everyone in vintage outfits and 40s music playing, and learn about the history from museum exhibits before it's recreated in the sky.

Southport, Merseyside, has hosted airshows since 1991 and 150,000 spectators a year make it the largest air show in the North West. Southport is a seafront display and costs are kept to a minimum with the show featuring a mixture of military and civilian aircraft and parachute displays. There are also assault courses if you're feeling fit!

Blackpool's free seafront display is held every August. No tickets, no queues to get in – just walk along the front and watch the airshow. You'll find food stalls, side shows and a festival atmosphere.

Sunderland Airshow is the largest free airshow in Europe. Held near Roker and Seaburn seafronts, it's been thrilling crowds since 1988. Normally in August, it attracts up to a million spectators a year.

Eastbourne International Airshow boasts a free, two-mile flying display along the seafront and has a host of stands and entertainment which continues long after the flying has finished.

Torbay's English Riviera Airshow is in June and usually kickstarts the UK's airshow season. The natural amphitheatre makes a unique location and over the years they've hosted many of the top military and civilian display teams.

If you'd like the whole RAF experience, head to the **RAF Cosford Airshow, Shropshire**. It's the only official RAF airshow and offers a six-hour flying display, over 100 static aircraft and over 150 stalls. There is plenty to see in the hangars and the RAF Cosford Museum. A ticketed display, it's raised over £1 million for charity.

NB: The Red Arrows are unable to display at every air show, so do check ahead if, or on which day, the team is performing before making plans.

Images: Shutterstock, Robyn Ferris, RAFAT Photographic Team

A TREE OF CELEBRATION

Prince Harry marking Oak Apple Day with the Chelsea Pensioners, 2019

Pop an oak leaf in your buttonhole this 29 May for Oak Apple Day, exhorts Matthew Groves

OF all the national celebrations we overlook, perhaps the most often missed is Oak Apple Day. While the ubiquity of eponymous public houses is indicative of how important the Royal Oak was, few such pubs take advantage of this red-letter day, and in some parts of the country it is unknown.

Oak Apple Day celebrates the restoration of monarchy to this sceptred isle. On 29 May 1660, Charles II was crowned and the Restoration through this Merry Monarch meant England revivified. Morris dancing, bell-ringing, the theatre, field sports, Christmas festivities as well as the House of Lords and the Book of Common Prayer took their proper place in the constitution after the oppressive yoke of the Puritan Commonwealth.

It was a reign of carnival and dissoluteness, with hedonism the spirit of the court. As Restoration poet the second Earl of Rochester, son of Charles's servant Wilmot who aided his successful escape, put it: "Restless he rolls about from whore to whore; A merry monarch, scandalous and poor."

As Prince of Wales, Charles II had been a fugitive under the Commonwealth regime and soldiers scoured the land for this heir to the Crown of Great Britain. His eventual escape to France, culminating in the Restoration, was legislated by Act of Parliament to be commemorated in "perpetuity" – this is until the public holiday was abolished by our Victorian forebears.

Derbyshire's festooned Garland King

It was Charles's adventures in avoiding the Roundhead state that led to the oak becoming a symbol of the celebrations. At the Battle of Worcester in 1651, the Royalists were defeated. Charles was a vital hostage for the Roundheads as he embodied the future survival of a Royal and Anglican Britain. Having fought to the last, he was lucky to escape from his HQ by the back door as the Roundhead commander entered by the front.

There were close calls before he reached safe exile. With a price on his head and his tall and swarthy appearance, hiding, disguise and high-speed flight were essential. It's said he had to play the role of a servant when getting a horse shod by a farrier. The two discussed politics, with Charles expressing the hope that the fugitive Stuart would be hanged! Though he made it to France, he would not return to his realm for nine years.

The significance of the Royal Oak occurred early on in his escape. The King turned to the network of his Roman Catholic supporters. Hair cropped and dressed in clothes of a farm labourer, he headed to Boscobel House, Shropshire. Here Charles, with his Royalist Colonel, William Careless, hid in the oak tree while Roundheads searched beneath them. So tired was the Prince that he slept propped up by the loyal Careless. Undetected, they were able to continue their flight.

Oak Apple Day is still celebrated in parts of the country like Castleton, Derbyshire, known as Garland Day, where the Garland King, hidden within a garland of flowers, rides through the town on horseback. In Moseley Old Hall, Staffordshire, a place the King hid during his escape, the story of his pursuit is re-enacted. At midday in Northampton a statue of King Charles II is adorned with oak leaves and a service of Holy Communion takes place. The day is marked at the Royal Hospital Chelsea, London, an institution owing its existence to the King. The Chelsea Pensioners gather to eat roast beef and drink beer, followed by plum pudding: an unusual choice for May, until you consider that the dessert was banned by the Commonwealth, linked as it was to Christmas festivities.

It was once custom to collect oak apples on the day, and wear oak leaves in one's lapel. Not to do so led to one's legs being whipped with nettles or having one's posterior grabbed – giving rise to the day's nickname of Pinch Bum Day! Its other name, Shick-Shack Day, is a corruption of an obscene way non-conformists to the rites of the Church of England were described, reminding us that Oak Apple Day is also about celebrating Anglicanism's Restoration as well as that of the monarchy.

The English monarchy goes back to the mists of time, linked to our ancient Christianity, which makes us who we are as a country. Oak Apple Day is a vital chapter in our national story. It helps, too, that it recalls quite the adventure and a triumph over the abolition of merry-making.

And if any Republicans need more persuading? Well, we could always brandish a few nettles!

Images: Shutterstock

Diana with the Queen Mother who was born when?

Princess Anne married whom in 1973?

A RIGHT ROYAL QUIZ

Our Royal History writer Paul James tests your knowledge of the Royal Family

Designer of the Royal wedding dress?

1. Who was the first Norman King of England?

2. In which year was Queen Elizabeth the Queen Mother born?

3. Including Prince Charles, how many Princes of Wales have there been?

4. Where were the remains of Richard III discovered in 2012?

5. Which Australian city was named after the Queen Consort of William IV?

6. Which monarch was the last Emperor of India?

7. What is the name of Princess Eugenie's first son, born 9 February, 2021?

8. Who did Princess Anne marry at Westminster Abbey in 1973?

9. Which monarch began the tradition of a Christmas Day broadcast?

10. Where did Prince William and Catherine Middleton first meet?

11. Which King was known as "The Hammer of the Scots"?
a) Edward I b) Henry III
c) Richard III

12. Where are the Crown Jewels kept?
a) Windsor Castle b) Westminster Abbey c) The Tower of London

13. How many children did Queen Victoria and Prince Albert have?
a) Seven b) Eight c) Nine

14. Who was the third wife of King Henry VIII?
a) Jane Seymour b) Anne of Cleves c) Catherine Howard

15. Where was Queen Elizabeth II born in 1926?
a) Buckingham Palace b) Royal Lodge, Windsor c) 17 Bruton Street, London

16. Who was the oldest monarch to ascend the throne?

The Duke and Duchess of Cambridge met where?

Henry VIII's third wife was whom?

Which King's mistress was Nell Gwyn?

a) William IV b) George IV
c) Edward VII

17. Where was Mary Queen of Scots executed?
a) Loch Leven Castle
b) Fotheringhay Castle c) Tower of London

18. Who designed the Queen's wedding gown in 1947 and Coronation dress in 1953?
a) Norman Hartnell b) Hardy Amies c) Angela Kelly

19. Which actress played the young Queen Elizabeth II in television's *The Crown*?
a) Claire Foy b) Olivia Colman
c) Imelda Staunton

20. Who was the only monarch to be born and die at Buckingham Palace?
a) Queen Victoria b) Edward VII
c) George VI

21. Which English monarch had the shortest reign?

22. Who was the last English monarch not to have been born in England?

23. Which King's mistresses included Nell Gwyn, Moll Davis, Lucy Walter and the Duchess of Portsmouth?

24. Since 1066 how many English monarchs never married?

25. Which branch of the Services did Princess Elizabeth join in 1944?

26. Which monarch's last words were reputedly "All my possessions for a moment of time"?

27. Including Boris Johnson, how many Prime Ministers have there been during the reign of Queen Elizabeth II?

28. Which monarch reigned between Henry I and Henry II?

29. Who is currently fourth in line to the throne?

30. Whose royal wedding was the first to be broadcast live on television?

Answers on page 106

TRUE OR FALSE?

31. Other than family pets as a child, the Queen's first corgi was called Susan.

32. Queen Victoria holds the record as England's longest reigning monarch.

33. Members of the Royal Family are not permitted to vote.

34. One of Queen Elizabeth II's titles is Duke of Lancaster.

35. Henry VIII was succeeded by his daughter Mary I.

36. Richard the Lionheart was the first monarch to live at Windsor Castle.

37. Henry III kept a polar bear at the Tower of London.

38. Queen Anne was so fat that her coffin was almost square.

39. Before he came to the throne, George VI competed in the Men's Doubles at a Wimbledon Tennis Championship.

40. Elizabeth I and Mary, Queen of Scots, never met.

The Fall

by Mary Bealey

The sun is sinking in the west,
Birds trill happily on
In that enveloping mellowness –
September is nearly gone.

Warmth still lingers in the air,
Soft gentle breezes blow.
Brown, golden, yellow leaves,
Not yet fallen, still do grow.

The boughs are all heavy,
Fruit ready to fall,
Delicious juicy pears,
Flat, against the wall.

Like crowned kings
At the garden gate,
Cupressus trees stand
Tall and straight.

Waving gently to and fro,
Majestic in their long green robe,
Whate'er the month shall come,
They never shed their load.

The sun sinks fast,
The day grows dim –
Soon flickering lights
Go on within.

At last, this lovely summer month,
In no time at all
Comes to an end:
It's called "The Fall".

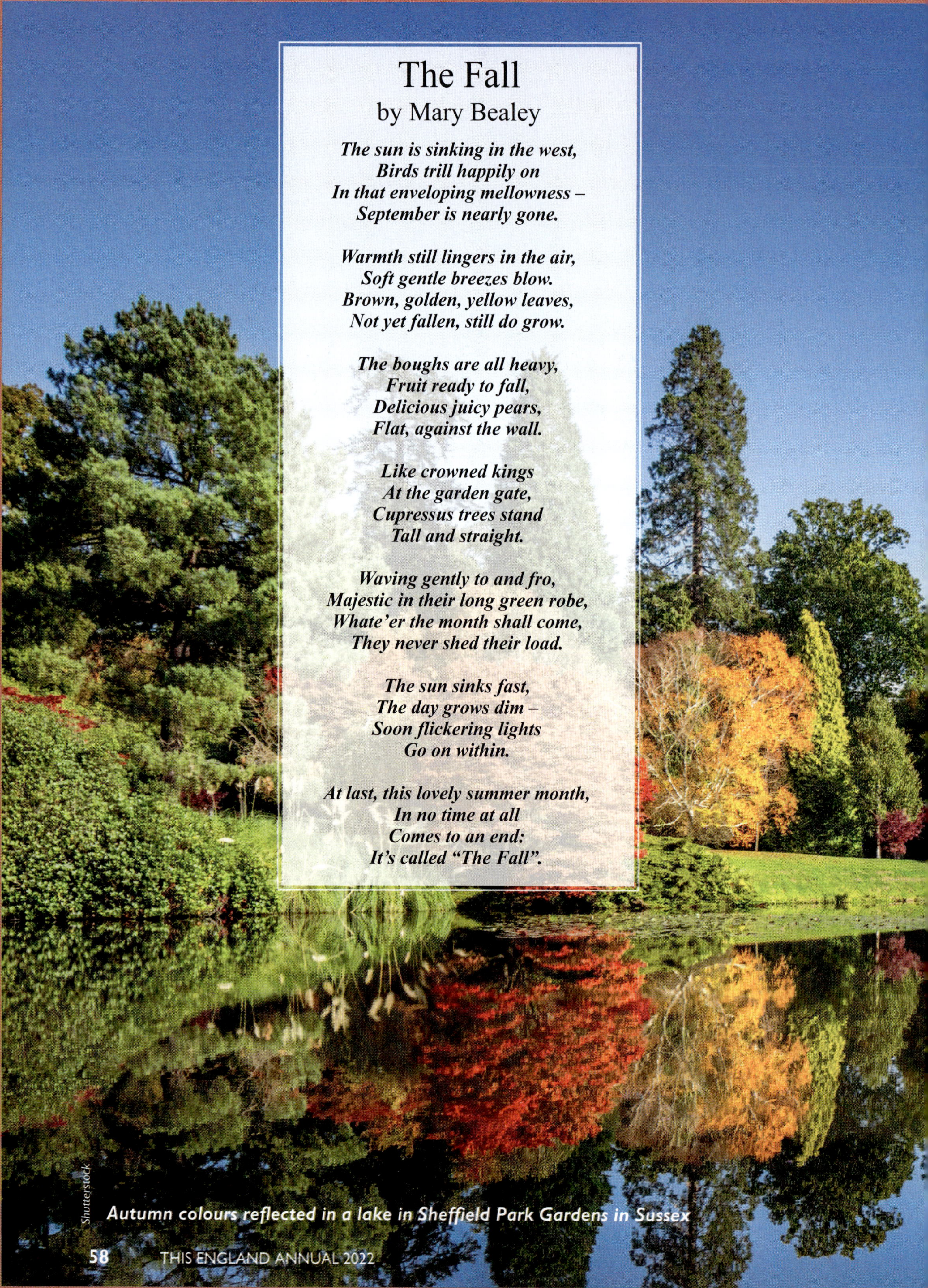

Shutterstock

Autumn colours reflected in a lake in Sheffield Park Gardens in Sussex

SUMMER TO AUTUMN

With top events, the BBC at 100 and remembering the genius of Ralph Vaughan Williams . . . >

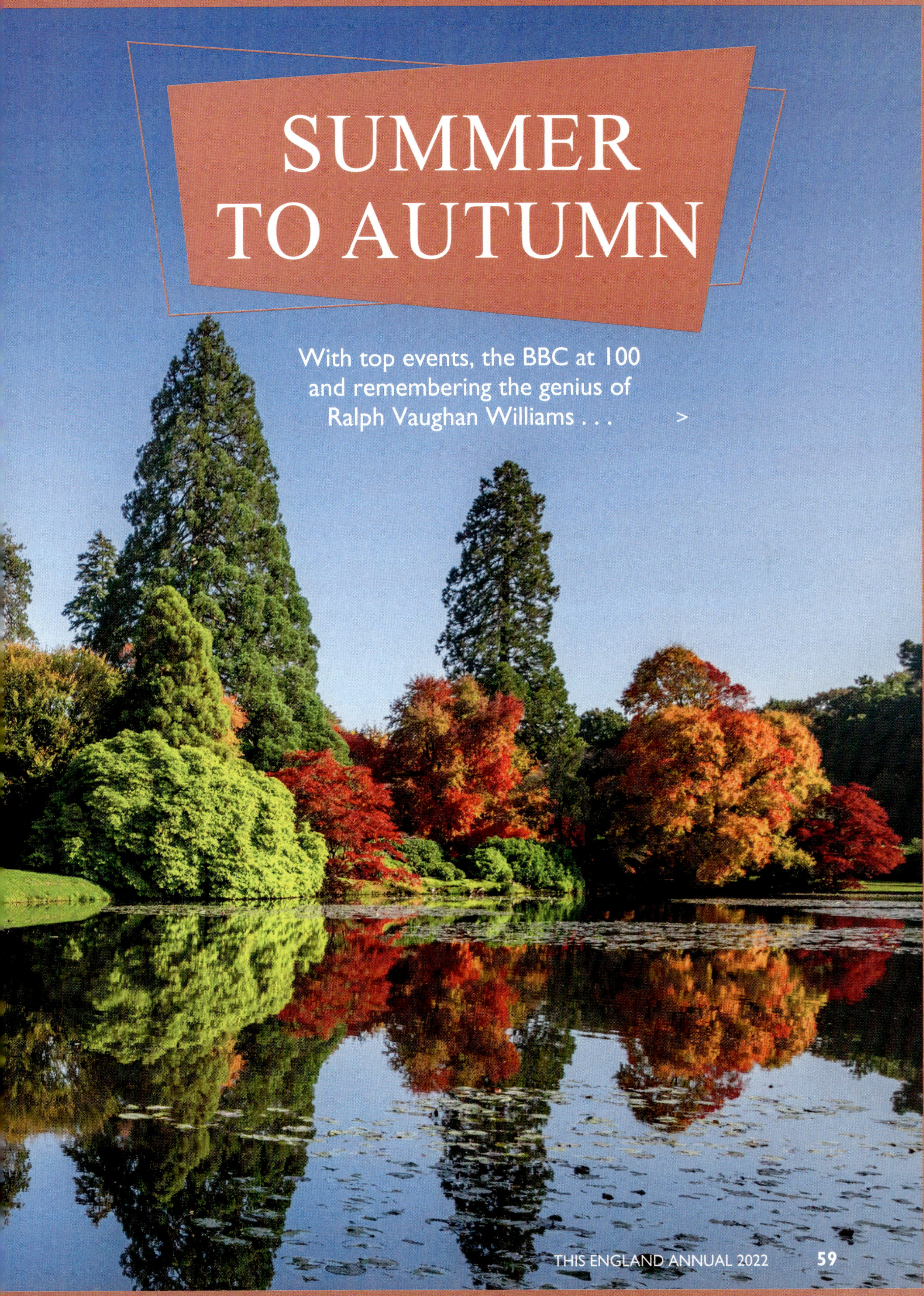

SUMMER TO AUTUMN

From snail racing to gurning, Katherine Sorrell gives us her pick of seasonal events along with some notable anniversaries

JULY 2022

THE COMMONWEALTH GAMES

From 28 July until 8 August, the Birmingham 2022 Commonwealth Games will be held in venues across Birmingham and the West Midlands. Around 4,500 athletes from 71 nations are set to come together to compete in everything from aquatics to wrestling. With 286 sessions, 19 sports and 283 medal events, it will be the biggest programme in the Games' history. Numerous records have been broken at the Commonwealth Games, known as the "Friendly Games", including Roger Bannister's sub-four-minute mile and Nicola Adams taking the first-ever gold medal in women's boxing. These games will be carbon neutral, with thousands of acres of forests created around Birmingham. **birmingham2022.com**

LAKE DISTRICT ELEVATION

It's the fifth anniversary of the Lake District, one of our most beautiful national treasures, being formally recognised by UNESCO as a World Heritage Site. This status which was given in July 2017, puts it right up there with the Taj Mahal, Great Barrier Reef, Easter Island and the Grand Canyon as one of the most iconic places on the planet.

The Lake District became a World Heritage Site in 2017

A CRICKET WORLD RECORD

Hedley Verity, record bowler

Yorkshireman Hedley Verity is regarded as one of the most effective slow left-arm bowlers in the history of English cricket, and it was in July 1932 that he achieved an incredible world record that still stands today: 10 wickets for 10 runs, in a county match between Yorkshire and Nottinghamshire. Verity played in four Ashes series, including the infamous "Bodyline" tour of Australia in 1932/33.

He died in 1943 at the age of just 38, after he was hit in the chest by shrapnel while leading his men against German troops in Sicily.

WORLD SNAIL RACING CHAMPIONSHIPS

The championships are part of the village fete in Congham, Norfolk, and they say that Congham is to snail racing what Newmarket is to horse racing. Simply select your garden snail and turn up. Ready, set . . . slow. **snailracing.net**

HENLEY ROYAL REGATTA

Set in picturesque Henley, this international rowing regatta, with more than 300 races, is both a sporting and social highlight. **hrr.co.uk**

RHS HAMPTON COURT PALACE GARDEN FESTIVAL

Explore the show gardens, admire the plants, shop for your outside space, have a picnic by Long Water or catch an expert talk to fill you with gardening inspiration, all set against the backdrop of the stunning Hampton Court Palace. **rhs.org.uk**

BBC PROMS
Eight weeks of the finest classical music brought to as many people as possible at affordable prices and in an informal atmosphere. The broad programme of music includes classical favourites, contemporary world premieres and family concerts. **bbc.co.uk/proms**

WHITSTABLE OYSTER FESTIVAL
A whole weekend dedicated to the oyster which starts with the Landing of the Oysters. There's food, drink and live music galore, an oyster parade, a "mud tug" and the building of "grotters" (small mounds of oyster shells lit by candles on the inside) on the beach at sunset. **whitstableoysterfestival.co.uk**

HENLEY FESTIVAL
As well as visual arts, top-class comedy and troupes of roving entertainers, there's fine dining and spectacular firework displays, plus an extensive programme of live music. Dress code is black tie. **henley-festival.co.uk**

ROLLING STONES' FIRST CONCERT

The young Stones in 1962

Hundreds of songs, scores of albums and an impressive number of world tours – The Rolling Stones have covered a lot of ground in 60 years, not to mention the public rows and changes in line-up. It all started on a summer's night back in 1962, when the regular Thursday night band at London's Marquee Club were invited to play a BBC live show. Their front man, one Mick Jagger, didn't go but persuaded the club's owner to let his new group play instead.

At the time, Jagger was quoted as saying: "I hope they don't think we're a rock 'n' roll outfit."

GARSTANG ICE CREAM FESTIVAL
National Ice Cream Day is on the third Sunday in July and Garstang, Lancashire, has everything ice-cream related you can possibly imagine, plus live entertainment and plenty of family fun. **facebook.com/garstangicecreamfestival/**

SILVERSTONE CLASSIC
The world's biggest classic motor racing festival, at Silverstone in Northamptonshire, features the cream of historic racing action, from Formula One and Sports Cars to GT and Touring Car grids. **silverstoneclassic.com**

NYETIMBER DORSET SEAFOOD FESTIVAL
Celebrating Dorset's links with the sea and its fishing communities, the UK's largest free seafood festival takes place around Weymouth's historic Old Harbour. Explore the journey from sea to plate in the Seafood Village, where you can try many different species of fish and shellfish from around 100 stalls. **dorsetseafood.co.uk**

COWES WEEK

Boats off the Isle of Wight

The oldest and largest annual sailing regatta in the world is now a key feature in the British sporting calendar, this year starting off on 30 July. The Isle of Wight event stages up to 40 daily races for around a thousand boats, and offers a mix of competitive sailing and social activities. The famous fireworks take place on the final Friday. **cowesweek.co.uk**

THE GAME FAIR
Or Glastonbury for the green wellie brigade. Expect air guns and archery, four-by-fours and fishing, gun dogs and game keeping, as well as a kitchen theatre, traditional crafts, shopping and a programme of displays and activities. The event is due to take place at Ragley Hall in Warwickshire. **thegamefair.org**

GREAT YORKSHIRE SHOW
This show is one of the biggest agricultural events in the English calendar, showcasing the best of British farming, food and the countryside at the Great Yorkshire Showground in Harrogate. **greatyorkshireshow.co.uk**

WINCHESTER HAT FAIR
The UK's longest-running festival of street theatre, comedy and music, but nothing to do with hats. It takes place across the historic city of Winchester during the first weekend of July. **hatfair.co.uk**

CHERTSEY BLACK CHERRY FAIR
First established in 1440, the Black Cherry Fair is held every year on the second Saturday in July. The lively community event in Chertsey, Surrey, features stalls, a music stage, live auction and fairground, plus a themed procession. **blackcherryfair.com**

>

AUGUST 2022

> ## GILBERT AND SULLIVAN FESTIVAL

This celebration of the works of the Victorian operatic duo, the country's most successful and enduring musical partnership, brings together a mix of professional and leading amateur groups, with performances in both Buxton and Harrogate, fringe events and cabarets. **gsfestivals.org**

CASTLE HOWARD PROMS

A memorable evening set against the glorious backdrop of Castle Howard in Yorkshire, one of England's finest historic houses. It includes popular classics, songs from musicals and all your flag-waving favourites, rounded off with a spectacular fireworks finale. **castlehoward.co.uk**

GREAT BRITISH BEER FESTIVAL

Britain's biggest beer festival, held at London's Olympia, brings you more than 1,000 real ales, ciders, perries and world beers, with live music and fabulous food. Tutored tastings and other educational experiences are also scheduled.
gbbf.org.uk

WEST DEAN CHILLI FIESTA

Find out how to use chillis in your cooking with talks and demonstrations, dance to live Latin music, learn about gardening or explore herb-inspired cocktail making . . . there are also children's activities, produce stalls and a fireworks finale. **westdean.org.uk**. For other chilli festivals, go to **chilliworld.com.**

THE 380TH ANNIVERSARY OF THE START OF THE ENGLISH CIVIL WARS

Also known as the Great Rebellion, the English Civil Wars began in August 1642, when King Charles I raised an army against the wishes of Parliament, ostensibly to deal with a rebellion in Ireland. Thus began almost 10 years of fighting between Royalists – also known as Cavaliers – and Parliamentarians, or Roundheads. It all ended with the execution of the King and the flight of his son, Charles II, to France, giving Oliver Cromwell and then his son Richard control over England, until the Restoration of the heir to the throne in 1660.

The opening scene of the English Civil War

HAPPY 150TH BIRTHDAY TO THE BANK HOLIDAY

Bank holidays were first introduced to England by the banker and politician Sir John Lubbock (an interesting chap who is alleged to have tried to teach his poodle how to read), who designated Easter Monday, the first Monday in August, 26th December, and Whit Monday in his Bank Holiday Bill of 1871. The first new paid holiday was taken in August 1872.

Bank Holiday river-based football at Bourton-on-the-Water

NOTTING HILL CARNIVAL

This joyful, diverse and vibrant community-led event has been taking over the streets of West London for five decades and is today second only to Rio's Carnival in size. Rooted in Caribbean culture, the bank holiday event is also reflective of modern London. **nhcarnival.org**

BRISTOL INTERNATIONAL BALLOON FIESTA

The incredible sight of hundreds of hot-air balloons filling the skies above Bristol is surely one not to be missed. Europe's largest annual balloon meeting attracts more than 130 participants from across the globe, with mass ascents and night-time illuminations.
bristolballoonfiesta.co.uk

EGTON BRIDGE GOOSEBERRY SHOW

One of just a handful of "goosegog" shows that remain in the UK, this is the the oldest and dates back to 1800. Each year, on the first Tuesday in August, members of the village's Old Gooseberry Society enter their biggest fruits into one of four classes. The heaviest gooseberry is determined by an apothecary scale that measures in drams and grains. In 2019 a new world record was set at 36 drams, 12 grains with a yellow "Millennium" berry.
egtongooseberryshow.org.uk

KETTLEWELL SCARECROW FESTIVAL

The Yorkshire scenery is the backdrop at this unusual festival which has scarecrows in every nook and cranny of the village, from famous celebrities and sports stars to topical characters and the downright quirky. It's said to be the biggest of its kind in the country and there is delicious homemade food served all day in the village hall.
kettlewellscarecrowfestival.co.uk

ROBIN HOOD FESTIVAL

Enjoyed by families and fans of the Robin Hood tales since 1984, this seven-day Nottinghamshire festival features live re-enactments, song, dance, storytelling, sword-fighting, archery and adventures with the outlaws. You'll find food and drink stalls, craft stands, demonstrations, medieval music, have-a-go archery and plenty of activities that will immerse you in the legends of Sherwood.
visitsherwood.co.uk

ARUNDEL FESTIVAL OF THE ARTS

This free community event in Arundel, West Sussex, is one of the largest multi-arts festivals in the South, taking place over 10 days around the August bank holiday each year. In addition to the extensive gallery trail, there's music, art, dance, drama, street entertainment, poetry, comedy, cabaret and more.
arundelfestival.co.uk

INTERNATIONAL BEATLEWEEK FESTIVAL

Fab Four fans converge on the Mersey for a week-long event that includes speakers, films, a giant Beatles collectibles market, performances from tribute bands and live music galore. Let it be.
internationalbeatleweek.com

FILM4 SUMMER SCREEN

As the sun sets over the London skyline, live DJs spin a soundtrack inspired by the upcoming screening and the Edmond J. Safra Fountain Court at London's Somerset House transforms into a beautiful open-air cinema. Just take a picnic and a cushion, and enjoy the show.
somersethouse.org.uk

KYNREN: AN EPIC TALE OF ENGLAND

Held at Flatts Farm in Bishop Auckland, Durham, every Saturday in the summer, this multi award-winning open-air performance employs a cast of 1,500 to reveal the history, myth and legend of England over 2,000 years. Expect invasions, royal splendour, wars, heroic sacrifice, daily life and seismic change. 11Arches Park is a brand-new daytime attraction in the park.
kynren.com

LYTHAM 1940S WARTIME WEEKEND

Vintage dress is essential

Lytham St Annes' popular event attracts visitors to Lancashire from all over the country. Roll back the decades and immerse yourself in the spirit of the wartime era with singing, dancing, big bands, educational talks, battle re-enactments, historic vehicles and vintage traders. **discoverfylde.co.uk/lytham1940s**

THE BRITISH FIREWORK CHAMPIONSHIPS

Fireworks over the Hoe

Each year six professional firework display companies are selected by draw to put on a 10-minute show for this spectacular two-night competition.
The natural amphitheatre of Plymouth Harbour and Sound is the ideal venue for large-scale pyrotechnics, and in addition there's plenty of entertainment on the Hoe with a funfair, live music, food and drink. **britishfireworks.co.uk**

THE SCARBOROUGH CRICKET FESTIVAL

One of the most historic sporting events in the world, the Scarborough Cricket Festival is an end-of-season series of cricket matches featuring Yorkshire County Cricket Club. It has been held in Scarborough since 1876 and, with the stands built right to the boundary edge, offers exceptional views and a unique atmosphere.
scarboroughcricketclub.co.uk

The Scarborough Cricket Festival: close to the action

>

SEPTEMBER 2022

20TH ANNIVERSARY OF A NOTABLE EARTHQUAKE IN ENGLAND

The 20-second tremor that struck the West Midlands town of Dudley on the night of 23 September 2002 was the biggest earthquake to hit England in a decade, measuring 4.8 on the Richter Scale. No-one was injured and only minor damage was caused, but 600 people dialled 999, several thousand called the emergency switchboard and 12 were said to have walked into the police station in their pyjamas.

Dudley: the scene of an earthquake that shocked residents

GRAIL QUEST RACE

The UK's only medieval-themed obstacle race takes place on Upton Bridge Farm in Long Sutton on the Somerset Levels. Racers take part in an 8 km race in which they must attack in the "Battle of Wessex" with the courage of a medieval knight, conquer "Agincourt" and trample, crawl or swim through the trenches. A medieval village has axe throwing, archery, weaponry displays, wholesome food and plenty of mead. **grailquestrace.co.uk**

LUDLOW FOOD FESTIVAL

Ludlow in Shropshire has been described as the gourmet capital of rural Britain, and its annual food festival involves talks, celebrity chef demos and tastings from more than 180 exhibitors in the grounds of Ludlow Castle.
foodfestival.co.uk

JANE AUSTEN FESTIVAL

The Regency era comes to life with this annual celebration of all things Austen, which features more than 80 events, from masked balls to country dances and tours of the city to dramatic performances. If you are wandering around Bath during this 10-day festival, from 9-18 September 2022, don't be surprised if you encounter characters from *Pride and Prejudice*, *Emma* or *Sense and Sensibility*.
janeaustenfestivalbath.co.uk

FAVERSHAM HOP FESTIVAL

This lively event recalls the traditional festivities associated with the hop harvest, and celebrates the Kent town's unrivalled hop heritage. It is now one of the largest free street festivals in the South East, and entertainment includes live music, arts and crafts, Morris dancers, a funfair and a traditional parade, as well as the Hop Blessing and special tours of Shepherd Neame, Britain's oldest brewer.
favershamhopfestival.org

PEARLY KINGS AND QUEENS HARVEST FESTIVAL

Celebrate the harvest with the Pearly Kings and Queens of London, decked out in their traditional finery. At the biggest event in the Pearly calendar, there's entertainment with maypole dancing and marching bands in front of the Guildhall, before a parade through the streets to St Mary-le-Bow Church for a service of thanksgiving. **pearlysociety.co.uk**

LAST NIGHT OF THE PROMS

The traditional finale of the Proms, usually on the second Saturday of September, to the eight-week summer seasons of classical concerts at London's Royal Albert Hall. **bbc.co.uk/proms**

60 YEARS AGO – THE LAST RUN OF THE PINES EXPRESS

The railway service that connected Manchester with Bournemouth first ran in 1910, and was named the Pines Express in 1927 because of the pine-tree-clad valleys of the south coast where it arrived. Trains ran daily throughout the year, but were busiest on summer Saturdays when they carried eager workers from the industrial north to their Dorset holidays. Its heyday was in the early 1950s, when it was much celebrated for both its picturesque route and its imposing carriages and restaurant car. However, on 8 September 1962 the last Pines Express to run on the Somerset & Dorset Joint Railway was hauled by the steam locomotive 92220 Evening Star, fittingly the last steam locomotive built by British Railways.

The "Pines Express" service finished in 1962

LONDON DESIGN FESTIVAL

This nine-day festival celebrates London's status as the UK's design capital and includes inspiring events all over the city. With venues from Bankside to West Kensington, designers present new ideas, products and new ways of thinking; visitors will also be impressed by a variety of eye-catching public installations. **londondesignfestival.com**

SHEEP DRIVE AND LIVERY FAIR

The practice of farmers driving their sheep across London Bridge into the City of London to sell at market died out by the early 20th century, but in 2013 the Worshipful Company of Woolmen arranged for Freemen of the City and their guests to officially drive sheep across the Thames once again. The event was so successful that it has continued, although now taking place on Southwark Bridge, which is closed to traffic for the day. **sheepdrive.london**

ALDEBURGH FOOD & DRINK FESTIVAL

This jam-packed weekend of food adventures at Snape Maltings celebrates the quality of local food, and includes tastings and demonstrations, workshops, discussions and shopping opportunities with more than 100 local producers. Two weeks of fringe events take place across Suffolk. **aldeburghfoodanddrink.co.uk**

SUSSEX BONFIRE SEASON

Bonfire celebrations take place in Sussex from early September to the end of November, marking Guy Fawkes Night and the burning of local martyrs. Sussex bonfire societies stage impressive torch-lit processions through the streets of historic towns and villages, featuring burning barrels, costumed marchers, thumping drums and (sometimes controversial) giant celebrity effigies. Enormous bonfires are the focal point. **lewesbonfirecelebrations.com**

WIDECOMBE FAIR

Run by volunteers to raise money for local causes, Widecombe Fair takes place on the second Tuesday of September each year in Dartmoor, Devon, and attracts visitors from far and wide. The epitome of a charming country fair, with everything from tug o' war to bale tossing, a dog and duck display to the ever-popular terrier race. **widecombefair.com**

EGREMONT CRAB FAIR

One of the world's oldest fairs, this celebrates the crab apple and traditional events mix with modern attractions, starting on Friday 16 September with a concert in Main Street. Saturday sees a parade in which apples are thrown from a cart, as well as local food and craft, ferret shows, equestrian events and the World Gurning Championships, where entrants compete to pull the ugliest face. **egremontcrabfair.com**

HERITAGE OPEN DAYS

See hidden places and try out new experiences in England's largest festival of history, architecture and culture. Every year in September, places across the country throw open their doors, allowing you to see inside historic homes, museum archives, castles, boats, gardens and all sorts of fascinating buildings, many of which are usually closed to the public. There are thousands of events that take place across the nation and all of them are free. **heritageopendays.org.uk**

Bombay Sapphire's gin distillery in Hampshire has taken part

MATLOCK BATH ILLUMINATIONS

This unique floating parade takes place every year on weekend evenings in September and October. Themed models are decorated by the Matlock Bath Venetian Boat Builders' Association with thousands of coloured lights, then mounted on rowing boats to be paraded along the River Derwent. As darkness falls, the brightly lit models appear to glide along the water by themselves. Expect a carnival atmosphere! **derbyshiredales.gov.uk/things-to-do/whats-on/matlock-bath-illuminations**

The illuminations at Matlock are reflected in the water

Images: Shutterstock & Alamy

ENGLISH BRIDGES

TYNE, NEWCASTLE

Poet, novelist and playwright Roger Harvey celebrates this iconic structure of his home city

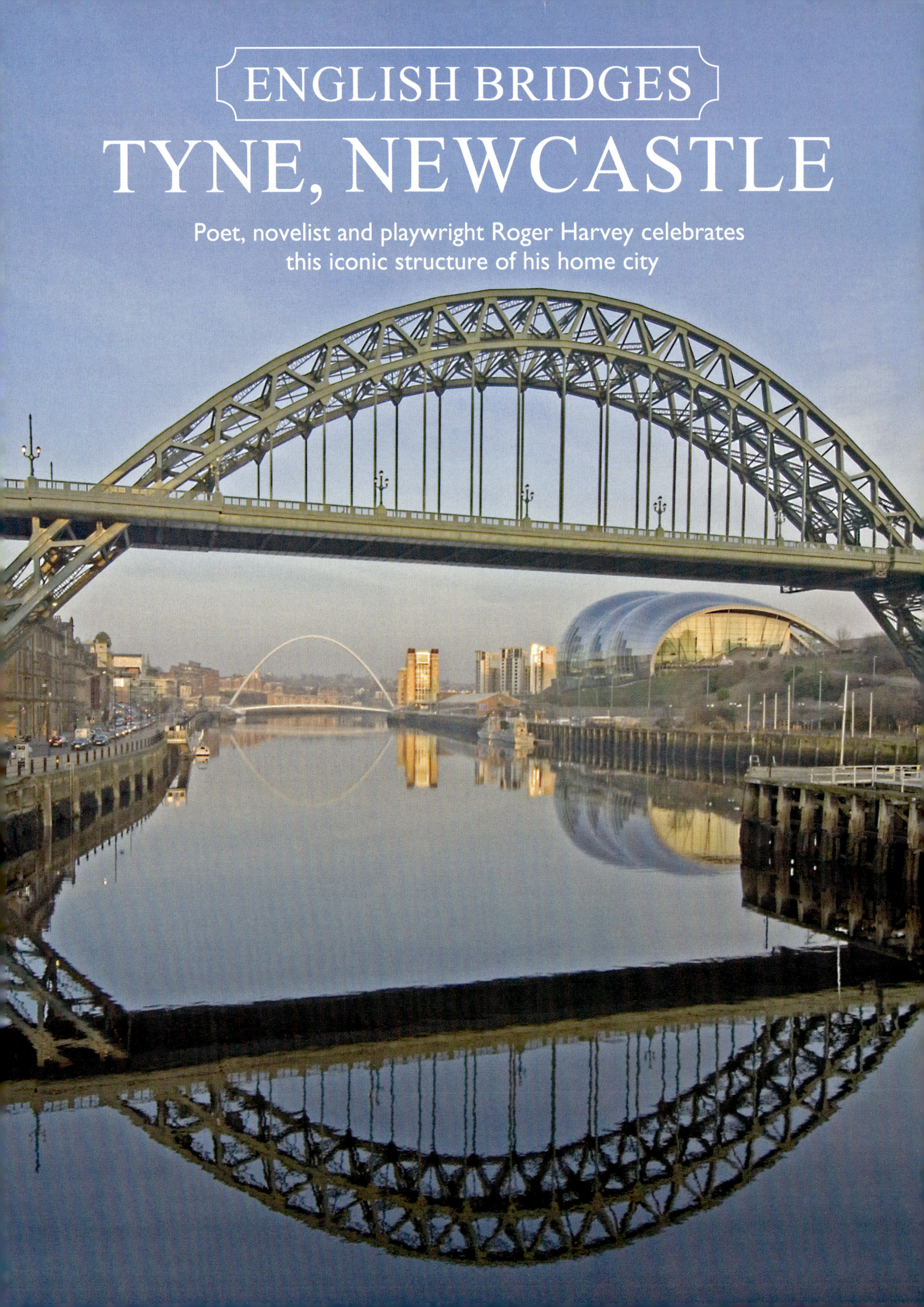

Lit & Phil Library

The Castle Keep

The Great North Museum

STRUCTURES like the Angel of the North may have become more emblematic of North East England, but since its opening by King George V and Queen Mary in 1928, nothing says "Newcastle" like the Tyne Bridge.

Famous photographs of its construction still sell as frameable prints and decorative tiles, it's used as a gigantic billboard for major sporting events, the Great North Run goes over it, and the Red Arrows line up with it. Throughout changing times, it is reassuringly impossible to ignore.

My only qualifications for writing about it are that my father was the first boy across it on a bicycle, and that 50 years later I wrote a poem about the Tyne which mentioned the bridge and was presented to the then Lord Mayor of Newcastle. Oh, yes, and I was born a Geordie.

Newcomers to the region may not realise it contains around 7,000 tonnes of Middlesbrough steel, nor that it takes about 12 tonnes of paint to cover it, but most will be struck by its similarity to a certain Antipodean erection of more gigantic proportions. This is no accident. Dorman Long, the celebrated civil engineer, tried out the design here before risking it across Sydney Harbour.

For most of my boyhood the bridge wore an overly fussy two-tone paint job, so it was with delight that I witnessed its repainting in the 1980s to that classic satin-finish green. We had a carefully repainted bridge to look up to, and now that both sides of the river have enjoyed redevelopment, the bridge has gained even greater visibility as a focal point of a great city.

But bridges aren't just for looking at – they are for crossing, and crossing the Tyne Bridge is one of the most symbolic acts a Geordie can perform. Up here, it takes the place of kissing one's native soil: a practice which never caught on in Newcastle owing to the state of the pavements and a reluctance to be thought "soft".

Crossing the bridge marks the beginning of an outward journey from Tyneside; re-crossing it means you're back home, and glad to be back. Even when crossing by another bridge, the Tyne Bridge exerts its influence: witness many a trainload of Novocastrians homeward-bound, marshalling bags as their carriages creak over the High Level or King Edward bridges saying "It's good to see the Tyne Bridge again."

So, next time you see it, cross it, or pass under it, reflecting on how it is to Newcastle what the Eiffel Tower is to Paris and those skyscrapers are to New York.

The River Tyne is crossed by other famous bridges, including the double-decker High Level and the Swing Bridge, but none carry the cachet of that famous green arch, least of all the relatively new Metro Bridge. Useful it may be, but it is ugly, too – although it does afford travellers spectacular views as trains rush from tunnel to tunnel.

And in that dazzling flash of riverscape, what do we notice first? The Tyne Bridge, of course. The green giant of Geordieland looks like spanning the river in style well into its next century.

THINGS TO DO IN NEWCASTLE

Newcastle Castle

Five minutes from the Tyne Bridge, this impressive structure was built on the site of the "new castle" constructed by Norman King William I, from which the city derives its name. The castle overlooks the city's quayside and regularly hosts cultural events, including film nights, live theatre, music, talks and more.

Newcastle Castle, Castle Garth NE1 1RQ; 0191 230 6300; newcastlecastle.co.uk

Great North Museum: Hancock

Located in central Newcastle, the Great North Museum: Hancock is a museum of natural history, archaeology, geology and world cultures. The building was built in 1884, with funds for the project raised by taxidermist John Hancock. Hancock's huge collection of British birds are still in the museum today.

Great North Museum: Hancock, Barras Bridge NE2 4PT; 0191 208 6765; greatnorthmuseum.org.uk

The Lit & Phil

Described as "Newcastle's exquisite secret library", the Lit & Phil has welcomed the public since 1825. The largest independent library outside London, it offers a wide selection of nearly 200,000 books, plus the largest music collection in the north of England.

The Lit & Phil, 23 Westgate Road NE1 1SE; 0191 232 0192; litandphil.org.uk

Images: Shutterstock, Alamy

MAGIC OF THE BROADCAST AGE

In 2022 the BBC celebrates its 100th birthday – Caroline Wheater explores the story of the world's leading public service broadcaster

"**THIS** is 2LO, Marconi House, London, calling," the announcer said on 14 November, 1922.

These words marked the BBC's first ever hour-long broadcast from Marconi House on the Strand, emitted via a radio transmitter so large that it filled a room. In homes in and around London, large "wireless" valve radios and crystal radio sets crackled into life as radio "hams" tuned in. So dawned Britain's broadcast age.

"It was a leap in the dark," says Robert Seatter, Head of BBC History. "Nobody really had any idea of what broadcasting could do. I always compare it to the internet revolution – it was all about the kit, the technology which came out of the telegraphy advances of the First World War."

Founded in October 1922, the British Broadcasting Company was a consortium of six radio firms, including the Marconi Company, which was granted a monopoly on broadcasting in Britain.

BBC microphone, 1940s

"The move was designed to prevent the kind of mayhem that had been seen in America, with unregulated radio stations popping up everywhere and with no way for the government to make money out of them," says Robert. The first General Manager of the new radio service was John Reith, a Scottish engineer and son of a church minister who proved to be a visionary leader. Like the other men who ran the fledgling BBC, he had served in World War I and bore a bayonet scar on his cheek as a reminder.

"Broadcasting was part of creating a better world and about good things coming from the horror of the devastation of the Great War," says Robert.

Reith's aim was to "entertain, inform and educate", and in his 1924 manifesto for the BBC, Broadcast over Britain, he pledged to get "the best of everything to the greatest number of houses".

"This new 'magic in a box' could transform ordinary lives. At the touch of a button people could have things they'd never had – popular dance music, classical music, the dramas of Shaw and Shakespeare, accurate time-keeping via the pips, and the news," explains Robert.

Reith fed the demand by coming up with the title for *Radio Times*, the magazine launched in 1923

November 1922
The BBC makes its first radio broadcast

February 1924
The "pips" are heard for the first time on the radio

January 1927
BBC becomes a public service broadcaster

November 1929
John Logie Baird airs his first trial TV broadcasts

May 1932
Broadcasting House is opened

December 1932
King George V starts BBC's Empire Service

November 1936
TV Service opens until it is halted by war in 1939

May 1937
George VI's coronation is first outside TV broadcast

January 1942
The first edition of *Desert Island Discs*

October 1946
Woman's Hour launches wih Alan Ivimey

1920s 1930s 1940s

Broadcasting House

Post-war favourite Muffin the Mule

The Forsyte Saga*, the BBC's first period drama*

that carried the strapline, "The Official Organ of the BBC". From its pages came joy – a typical schedule in the 1920s might include *The Daily Service*, music from the *BBC Dance Orchestra*, and *Children's Hour*.

The British Broadcasting Company's monopoly on broadcasting ran out at the end of 1926, but Reith, with a strong belief in public service broadcasting, proposed that it became a public corporation instead, overseen by a board of governors. Rather than profits driving programming, it would be public interest – in music, drama and everything else lapped up by radio licence holders whose numbers had grown from 30,000 in 1922 to around two million.

The government agreed, and in January 1927 a Royal Charter established the British Broadcasting Corporation, with Sir John Reith (he was a knight by then) appointed Director-General.

Says Lewis Pollard, curator of TV and Broadcast at the National Science and Media Museum in Bradford: "It was a pioneering move for the BBC to give the public a stake in what it was doing, and has made it the cultural touchstone it is today, the core media institution in the UK."

In the early Thirties, the BBC moved into a purpose-built centre, Broadcasting House on Portland Place (recently given an overhaul for the 21st century). The metaphor of radio as magic was reflected in Eric Gill's large carved statue of Prospero and Ariel above the imposing front entrance, both magical symbols in Shakespeare's last play *The Tempest*.

In 1932 the Empire Service (renamed the World Service in 1965) brought the globe together as it reached out around the British Empire. In King George V's Christmas message, written by Rudyard Kipling, he said: "Through one of the marvels of modern science, I am enabled, this Christmas Day, to speak to all my peoples throughout the Empire". His son, Edward VIII, announced his abdication live from Windsor Castle in December 1936.

Britain's greatest gift to the world in the 20th century

Kofi Annan, former UN Secretary General, on the BBC's World Service

At the start of World War II in 1939, the National and Regional Programmes merged to become the Home Service, broadcasting news and entertainment to keep up morale. Prime Minister Neville Chamberlain announced Britain's declaration of war on Germany on the Home Service and his successor Winston Churchill made many rallying speeches.

"Over 1,000 coded messages were broadcast in French from the BBC to relay information to the French Resistance," adds Robert. >

July 1948
London Olympics is the biggest outdoor radio and TV operation of its time

January 1950
Listen with Mother for children starts on the radio

June 1953
The Coronation of Queen Elizabeth II is screened live on TV

November 1954
Hancock's Half-Hour launches and runs until 1961

1950s

October 1958
The children's show *Blue Peter* launches

1960s

June 1960
Television Centre opens in White City

January 1964
Top of the Pops starts with The Rolling Stones

April 1964
BBC Two, the UK's 3rd TV channel begins

September 1967
Radio 1 goes live with Tony Blackburn

September 1967
The Home Service relaunches as Radio 4

The Beatles on Top of the Pops, *1966*

David Attenborough's Life on Earth, *1979*

> They could be bizarre, such as "Le lapin a bu un apéritif" – "The rabbit drank an aperitif" – but undoubtedly saved Allied lives.

Although John Reith's focus was radio rather than television, the BBC Television Service (renamed BBC One in 1964) began broadcasting to Londoners from its Alexandra Palace studios in 1936 – drama, sport, outside broadcasts and even lifestyle programmes such as *In The Garden*, a forerunner of *Gardeners' World*. With production halted during World War II – it was feared the tall transmitter mast would be used by the Luftwaffe to navigate London – the Television Service roared back into life in 1946 with popular puppet Muffin the Mule.

"It was the Coronation of Queen Elizabeth II in June 1953 that boosted television's popularity," says Lewis. The event, broadcast live with commentary by Richard Dimbleby, saw friends and neighbours crowding around black and white televisions to watch proceedings on the nine-inch wide screens. "It was the big moment of post-war glamour, showcasing a

I hadn't the remotest idea as to what broadcasting was

John Reith, first Director General of the BBC

beautiful young Queen and her handsome consort," says Robert. Adverts for televisions even encouraged people to "put an H aerial on your roof and see how many friends you make".

Another visionary, Director-General Hugh Carleton Greene, (the brother of author Graham Greene) "opened up the windows to let in new air" at the BBC in the 1960s. The new Television Centre in White City – the world's first – opened in 1960 and was dubbed a "television factory".

"The BBC became more adventurous," says Robert, as satirical programmes such as *That Was The Week That Was* marked the end of the age of deference.

A hive of creative activity, the BBC attracted top talents, such as producer Biddy Baxter, the brains behind *Blue Peter*, and Verity Lambert, producer of *Doctor Who*, and there followed a slew of original programming, from *Play School* to *Top of the Pops* to *The Forsyte Saga*, the 1967 costume drama that launched a thousand others.

"This is the start of the inter-generational aspect of the BBC,

April 1975
Classic sitcom *The Good Life* begins its run

September 1979
Sir Robin Day chairs the first *Question Time*

July 1981
Royal wedding of Charles and Diana had a global reach

November 1992
Ab Fab is launched with its comedic prowess

November 1995
Panorama interview with Diana is shown

1970s 1980s 1990s

January 1979
Attenborough starts *Life on Earth*

November 1980
Children in Need telethon starts for the first time

December 1986
EastEnders 30mil tune in to see Den divorce Angie

September 1995
DAB or digital radio starts to roll out

November 1997
BBC News 24 starts; a month later the BBC website goes live

BBC BROADCASTS THAT BROKE THE MOULD

***The Archers*, Home Service, January 1951**
The Archers, the world's longest-running soap opera about the fictional village of Ambridge, was trialled on the Midlands Home Service for five episodes before going national. It was devised to promote good agricultural practice and soon became a national institution.

***Royal Family*, BBC1, June 1969**
The fly-on-the-wall documentary, *Royal Family*, produced by Richard Cawston, showed the Queen and Prince Philip at leisure and carrying out state duties. A joint production by the BBC and ITV, it was watched by 30 million in Britain, with 350 million viewers worldwide.

***Live Aid*, BBC2, July 1985**
Live Aid was a multi-venue rock concert organised by Bob Geldof and Midge Ure aiming to raise money to feed the world at a time of famine in Ethiopia. Broadcast to an estimated 400 million people across 60 countries, it was one of the largest satellite link-up, showcasing 58 bands during 16 hours of music.

***Planet Earth*, BBC1, March 2006**
The most expensive nature series ever commissioned by the BBC, this award-winning 11-part documentary narrated by Sir David Attenborough was filmed over five years, across 64 countries. The HD sequel *Planet Earth II*, was out in 2016, while *Planet Earth III* is due to air in 2022.

allowing parents and children to share enjoyment of the same series," explains Lewis. It is a factor described as "huge long strands of social glue" by Robert. BBC radio had a refresh, too, with Radio 1, 2, 3 and 4 being formed – the core radio stations that still keep us company on the online audio service BBC Sounds today.

With the Corporation's production framework in place, the 1970s, 80s and 90s were a golden age for current affairs, drama, light entertainment and music. Viewers watched Robin Day chair *Question Time* and fell in love with *The Good Life*'s Tom and Barbara. They made a legendary date with Bob Geldof's *Live Aid* and giggled at the whimsical tale of *The Fall and Rise of Reginald Perrin*. The BBC became renowned for its beautifully rendered costume dramas, exemplified by the 1995 version of Jane Austen's *Pride and Prejudice* starring Colin Firth as that Mr Darcy and Jennifer Ehle as Miss Elizabeth Bennet.

The BBC's world-renowned Natural History Unit came to prominence with Sir David Attenborough's 13-part series *Life on Earth* in 1979 and one of the nation's greatest communicators has since become a household name. Lewis Pollard comments: "His series *Blue Planet II*, first televised in 2017, was so hard-hitting that it caused the 'Blue Planet effect', making people more conscious about the harmful effects of single-use plastics and of the importance of sustainability."

> I always used to consider myself a failure until I appeared on *Top of the Pops*
>
> **Jarvis Cocker of Pulp**

In the 21st century, quality continues to stream out of the BBC, on television, online and on radio, bolstered by worldwide sales of *Top Gear*, *Strictly Come Dancing* and *Doctor Who*, programmes that seem to define Britishness.

"Our national memory is defined by the BBC in a way that didn't exist when broadcasting wasn't there," Robert says. "It reflects society and also changes it; sometimes it's ahead and sometimes its behind. Because it has such wide output, from news to dramas to sport, it's very complex, but society is very complex.

"One hundred years of the BBC is 100 years of Britain."

2000s

May 2004
Strictly Come Dancing sashays on to BBC1 on Saturday evenings

February 2005
The Apprentice launches, with Sir Alan Sugar

July 2007
The innovative BBC iPlayer launches

December 2009
Sir Terry Wogan signs off from his Radio 2 breakfast show after 27 years

2010s

August 2010
The first series of the *Great British Bake Off* begins

August 2012
BBC's coverage of the Olympics reaches 51 million

December 2017
Jodie Whittaker becomes the first female Dr Who

February 2019
Antiques Roadshow is now 40 years old

2020s

2020-21
BBC helps the nation's children do lockdown homework

2 November 2022
The BBC is due to celebrate its 100th birthday!

WHERE IN ENGLAND?

Identify the location of these English scenes; answers on p106

1 **In which county will you find the Singing Ringing Tree sculpture?**

2 **In which Surrey university town will you find the Millmead Lock?**

3 **It's the county town of Lancashire, but where is this?**

4 **The Minack Theatre is one of the most stunning in the world. In which county will you find it?**

5 **The Needles Lighthouse is off the coast of where?**

6 **Which English city has more canals than Venice?**

7 **It's England's second largest county and famous for its windmills. Which county is it?**

8 **This cathedral city sits on the River Wye. Where is it?**

9 **The Golden Ball on the Church of St Lawrence sits in the Chiltern Hills in which county?**

10 **This majestic castle is in which Cumbrian city?**

11 **The River Great Ouse runs through five counties. Which are they?**

12 **Said to be the longest Georgian crescent in Europe, which city claims Royal York Crescent?**

13 **The spectacular Blenheim Palace sits on the edge of which town in Oxfordshire?**

14 **Which seaside town's beach sits near the country's largest container port?**

Images: Shutterstock and Alamy

SONG OF THE SKYLARK

In the 150th anniversary year of Ralph Vaughan Williams's birth, Rebecca Franks celebrates his most beloved composition

Vaughan Williams by Gerald Festus Kelly, oil on canvas, 1958-61

IT begins with an atmospheric soft haze, the orchestra conjuring a quiet stillness. A solo violin enters, tracing a line that inexorably rises, decorated with gentle flutters and falls. On it climbs, higher and higher, until at its highest point, the violin melts into a pure, lilting melody.

This is the start of *The Lark Ascending*, a romance for violin and orchestra inspired by George Meredith's eponymous 1881 poem about the song of a skylark.

"He rises and begins to round, He drops the silver chain of sound," quoted its composer, Ralph Vaughan Williams, on the score. "For singing till his heaven fills, 'Tis love of earth that he instils."

The Lark Ascending holds a special place in Britain's national imagination today. It has topped the Classic FM Hall of Fame chart ten times since 1996.

In 2011, listeners of BBC Radio 4's *Desert Island Discs* voted it their favourite piece with which to be cast away. Since the turn of the millennium, it has been performed almost every other summer at the *BBC Proms*, and in 2020, amid the tribulations of the pandemic, it was played at a landmark *Last Night of the Proms*.

"Time seems to stop in this piece and I think that really strikes a chord with modern life, with its noise, technology and pressure. The audience is allowed to go completely to another place," reflects Jennifer Pike, one of Britain's leading violinists, and a devotee of the piece. "When I play it, I don't try to sound exactly like a bird; it's more I try to capture a quite physical sensation, of being lifted out of something – that sense of escape."

For a piece that is so popular, it's surprising that there's no definitive account of how it came about. We know that Vaughan Williams first wrote *The Lark Ascending* in 1914, then in 1919 he returned to the piece and revised it. The rest of the story we can only glimpse.

One enticing but probably apocryphal tale suggests that in the summer of 1914 he was walking on cliffs overlooking the Channel, where British troops were on their way to war, when he paused to write a tune in his notebook. He was promptly waylaid by a Boy Scout who thought he was a spy, and was marched to a police station. Yet, in another version of these events, the composer was scribbling a lecture on Purcell when the music came to him.

More certain is the influence of

Top: Queen's Hall, 1901
Middle left: Musical prodigy Marie Hall
Middle right and bottom left: With Malcolm Sargent who regularly performed his work
Bottom right: As an ambulance driver, 1915

violinist Marie Hall, to whom he dedicated the piece. One critic noted in 1928 that Vaughan Williams had been struck by Hall's "delicacy and brilliancy of playing during an evening spent with a friend in Italy", and later *The Times* suggested Hall's performances of solo Bach – she often played Bach's *Chaconne* – had been an important catalyst.

Hall was by this point internationally renowned, a prodigy from Newcastle who had wowed the public at her London debut in 1903, at the age of 19. Sadly no recording of her playing *The Lark Ascending* exists, although an abridged version of Elgar's *Violin Concerto* showcases the acute beauty of her playing.

War put everything on hold. Vaughan Williams enlisted in the Royal Army Medical Corps, and was sent to France as a stretcher-bearer. It was only when he was discharged that he returned to the piece, reworking it and readying it for performance. *The Lark Ascending*'s first flight took place on 15 December, 1920, in Shirehampton Public Hall, Bristol.

"It's quite a small and humble venue," explains Pike, who performed at a concert marking the piece's centenary, "There's a little plaque on the door for Marie Hall, and it was magical to think that a hundred years before she had played there. And I was thinking, which seat was Vaughan Williams in?"

The composer had been among the audience, and though there were no reviews of the occasion, the programme explained he had arranged the version for violin and piano premiered that night.

"It's very different," reflects Pike. "The piano has this percussive quality, and it feels like church bells."

The full premiere for violin and >

"The audience is allowed to go completely to another place": violinist Jennifer Pike

> an orchestra of strings, woodwind, two horns and triangle took place the following June at Queen's Hall in London, (the venue was later destroyed in the Blitz), with Hall again the soloist, accompanied by the British Symphony Orchestra and conducted by Adrian Boult.

The Lark Ascending made an instant impression. *The Westminster Gazette* believed it to be "one of the happiest things that the composer has ever done . . . full of melody and grace, of ease and spontaneity". *The Times*'s critic noted that the piece "showed serene disregard of the fashions of today or yesterday. It dreams its way along . . . the music is that of the clean countryside, not of the sophisticated concert-room". *The Illustrated London News* felt that "Hall's coldly beautiful style was exactly the right interpretation for [the work's] serene and remote sense of contemplation".

Vaughan Williams had written a piece that felt at once strikingly new and utterly familiar. His total success at transforming a poetic idea into music was matched by vivid word painting and effortless evocation of an English landscape.

"It's such a popular work, but that often masks the originality of it," says Pike. "We forget, for instance, that those three cadenzas at the beginning for solo violin, with no restraint, no bar lines, have been written with this really forward-thinking idea of just letting the violin feel like it's improvising."

There were other distinctive touches, too: folk-song-like melodies, modal harmonies, rhapsodic freedom, imaginative orchestral colours.

That he tapped into a communal yearning for a rural idyll was not luck but design. Vaughan Williams believed that "the art of music above all arts is the expression of the soul of the nation". He felt that musicians should be useful people and had a strong work ethic from childhood. Born in 1872 in Gloucestershire with, in his words, "a very small silver spoon in his mouth", Ralph Vaughan Williams's heritage was one of intellectualism, industry and artistry.

He was a direct descendant of the Darwins and Wedgwoods. He grew up in Surrey, learned the piano, violin, organ and, later, viola, and he was just six when he wrote his first piano piece, *The Robin's Nest*.

At the Royal College of Music he studied with two important figures in British music, Charles Stanford and Hubert Parry, and he also took degrees in Music and History at Trinity College, Cambridge.

In 1903, Vaughan Williams stepped out on his own path when he began collecting folk songs. Over the next decade he noted down almost 800 songs and carols from 21 English counties, some of which made it into the *English Hymnal*, which he edited from 1904-06. Compiling tunes for this landmark volume was, he said, "a better musical education than any amount of sonatas and fugues".

By the time he wrote *The Lark Ascending*, Vaughan Williams had found his voice. But while the piece took on its own life – taken up by over 40 violinists in its first 20 years, and recorded nearly 200 times over the following decades, including by Nigel Kennedy, Tasmin Little and Jennifer Pike – the composer continued to explore new ground.

"The one thing about *The Lark Ascending*'s popularity that isn't good is that Vaughan Williams wrote so many other interesting works. He has so many different sides," says Pike.

He became, arguably, Britain's greatest symphonist, penning a cycle of nine symphonies that span much of his creative life and display huge emotional range. While *The Lark Ascending* is often seen as an elegy for a lost past, it's actually his third symphony – the *Pastoral Symphony* of 1922 – that is a war requiem in all but name. The symphony's four movements are predominantly slow, a daring move, while the haunting passages for solo trumpet and wordless soprano conjure a lone bugler and a lamenting mourner.

In 1952, six years before he died, he composed his final major work.

"I was definitely shocked by the *Violin Sonata*, in a really good way," says Pike. "It's full of passion and anguish, and is uncompromising."

The last of the three movements is its crowning glory.

"It has this fantastic chorale, this theme and variations that build into this huge structure, like a cathedral," says Pike. "And then at the end the violin has this cadenza, and he's nodding back. It's this little memory of *The Lark Ascending*."

It seems however far Vaughan Williams voyaged in style and subject matter, he never forgot his beloved skylark.

Images: Alamy, Shutterstock

HORTICULTURAL HEROES

Gillian Thornton investigates three plant pioneers from Hertfordshire

THE Hertfordshire market town of St Albans has many claims to fame. Founded by the Romans as Verulamium, it was later renamed in honour of Alban, England's first Christian martyr. A church was built on the spot where Alban was beheaded for his faith, and by the Middle Ages the town was thriving on revenue from pilgrims and travellers heading north from London.

In the 12th century, local cleric Nicholas Breakspear became the only Englishman ever to hold the office of Pope, as Adrian IV, and, in 1455, the Wars of the Roses kicked off here in its first battle, which lasted just half an hour. But fast forward to more recent times and both St Albans and its near neighbour Harpenden have earned a unique place in the international world of plants. Today, visitors can still enjoy places connected with three green-fingered local residents who made their mark in the fields of world agriculture, exotic orchids and popular gardening, not to mention a legendary international golf trophy!

Rothamsted Farm, Harpenden

John Bennet Lawes in 1882

SIR JOHN BENNET LAWES

Agricultural scientist and entrepreneur

From small beginnings in the Home Counties of England, the research begun by John Bennet Lawes into fertilisers and crop growth has transformed the lives of farming communities across the globe. Born in 1814, Lawes was a scientist, entrepreneur and benefactor who founded the world's first agricultural research institution, now known as Rothamsted Research, at his home, Rothamsted Manor.

Lawes was educated at Oxford and on graduating ordered one of the bedrooms at the manor to be fitted out as a laboratory. Here he undertook experiments in pots before progressing to field trials, determined to prove the importance of phosphorus in plant nutrition.

Lawes discovered that bones treated with sulphuric acid produced a more soluble phosphorus fertiliser which greatly increased crop yields, and thanks to this superphosphate, patented in 1842, he constructed the world's first commercial fertiliser factory at Deptford.

In 1843, Lawes founded Rothamsted Experimental Station in Harpenden, in partnership with scientist Joseph Henry Gilbert, simultaneously launching the first of their "Classical Experiments". Today, visitors can follow a trail across the estate taking in historic field experiments and high-tech gadgets for recording insect data, all explained on a series of information panels.

On the way, walkers pass the Broadbalk experiment, set up to test the impact of inorganic fertilisers and organic manures on wheat yields and soil fertility. The oldest continuous arable experiment in the world, Broadbalk is still

Heath & Heather *catalogue, 1930s*

SAMUEL RYDER

Pioneer of the penny seed packet

You don't need to be a golfer or sports fan to be familiar with the Ryder Cup, but few people know the origins of this prestigious trophy, nor the impact its founder had on popular gardening.

Born in 1858 near Preston in Lancashire, Samuel Ryder, the son of a market gardener, initially joined his father's business. With business ideas of his own, Ryder moved to St Albans in 1895 with his wife, attracted by the town's rail links. Ryder identified a new market for selling seeds by post, especially to the working classes. Starting from his garden shed, he began selling "penny packets" of fruit and veg seeds: the first person to bring gardening to a mass market. Out of respect for his father, he called his business Ryder & Son, Samuel himself being the son. As the business grew, Samuel moved to new homes and premises around St Albans with his family.

A devout non-conformist, Ryder was appointed mayor of the city in 1905, and in addition to Ryder & Son, he set up Heath & Heather herbal shops with his brother, later to become part of Holland & Barrett. This took a toll on Ryder's health, so he joined the city's Verulam Golf Club for fresh air and exercise. It wasn't long before his entrepreneurial flair asserted itself and, in 1926, he suggested a tournament to turn an individual sport into a team game between nations.

The first Ryder Cup was presented to the USA in 1927, and the 44th will take place for the first time in Italy, from September 2022. A replica of the cup stands today in his old clubhouse in St Albans.

Today, visitors to St Albans can follow his progress as businessman, churchman and local politician on a self-guided walking trail, available from the Samuel Ryder Foundation at sryder.com. The "nine-hole" version of the Samuel Ryder Trail involves a stroll round St Albans city centre and includes his former head office on Holywell Hill. Now a Clarion Collection Hotel, its Arts and Crafts style includes a sweeping staircase and magnificent stained-glass dome. There's more stained glass next door in Ryder's former Exhibition Hall, an Art Deco building with a carved roof where visitors could see flower-beds sown with plants grown from Ryder's Seeds. On the route is the Old Town Hall, now St Albans Museum and Gallery, where Samuel presided over meetings and court appearances.

The other nine holes of the trail take walkers beyond the centre to Hatfield Road Cemetery, where Ryder was buried in 1936. It's also the resting place of orchid pioneer Frederick Sander, and barely five miles from Sir John Bennett Lawes's grave in Harpenden.

Samuel Ryder presents the Ryder Cup to George Duncan, captain of the British team

used by scientists working on plant nutrition. Also on the route is Park Grass, launched in 1856 to investigate how fertilisers and manure could improve hay yields. Today it is regarded as the oldest ecological experiment in existence.

In 1854, Lawes was elected a Fellow of the Royal Society for his investigations in the field of agricultural chemistry, and in 1882 Queen Victoria honoured him with a baronetcy, 18 years before his death at Rothamsted Manor. The Grade I listed property is open for occasional tours and events.

Rothamsted Manor

Lawes rests in St Nicholas churchyard in Harpenden, just feet away from his long-time friend and collaborator Sir Joseph Gilbert, and a short walk from eminent Rothamsted botanist Katherine Warington, who died in 1993. It's easy to imagine them all at work as you follow the walking trail, past the modern laboratories and across the estate that still contributes vital data to 21st-century agricultural scientists across the globe. **enjoystalbans.com/things-to-do/outdoors; rothamstedenterprises.com**

Frederick Sander enjoying time with his wife and grandchildren

FREDERICK SANDER
Orchid King of St Albans

George Street is one of St Albans' most picturesque and popular streets with its boutiques, antiques shops and restaurants beneath half-timbered facades. Few people today are aware that this was the birthplace of a horticultural business that attracted wealthy customers and crowned heads of Europe to the city in the 19th century.

In 1876, 39-year-old plantsman Frederick Sander purchased a seed merchant's shop on George Street. Born in Bremen, he came to England aged 18, working as a nurseryman in Forest Hill. Here he met Czech plant hunter Benedict Roezel, and when Roezel needed an agent to sell his plants, Sander saw an opportunity.

Soon, Roezel was able to retire to Prague, so Sander concentrated on growing orchids, buying an area of land just outside the town centre in 1881. He built a large home and set up a four-acre nursery where some 60 glasshouses replicated climates varying from the Tropics to the Himalayas.

By 1894, Frederick had set up a larger orchid nursery in Bruges, also stocking azaleas, palm trees, lilies and begonias. But Europe's aristocracy and monarchs still came to St Albans to buy flamboyant flowers to adorn their country mansions and townhouses. The finest blooms cost thousands of guineas, but Sander brought orchids within the reach of modest buyers. In the 1880s and '90s, two million plants passed through the St Albans operation, earning him the nickname "The Orchid King".

At its peak, Sanders Orchids employed 23 plant hunters, working in difficult and dangerous conditions across the globe. Sander published *Reichenbachia*, a series of giant leather-bound books with detailed orchid descriptions and life-size illustrations painted by his son-in-law Henry Moon.

Sander was honoured with the Belgian Insignia of Chevalier of the Order of the Crown in 1913, but the outbreak of war began the decline of his empire. He died in Bruges in 1920, following an operation, and his body was brought back to St Albans, laid to rest alongside Henry Moon who had died 15 years before.

Sanders Orchids traded until the death of Frederick's last surviving son, closing for good in 1957. Today, a primary school stands on the site of the family home, but Frederick's legacy lives on in nurseries, florists and garden centres across the world. Once exclusive to wealthy collectors, orchids became affordable to the masses thanks to Sander, the man who helped put a touch of the exotic on the windowsills of the world. **fleetvillediaries.org**

Odontoglossum insleayi splendens, from Sander's Reichenbachia

Images: Shutterstock, Alamy, Gillian Thornton unless stated otherwise

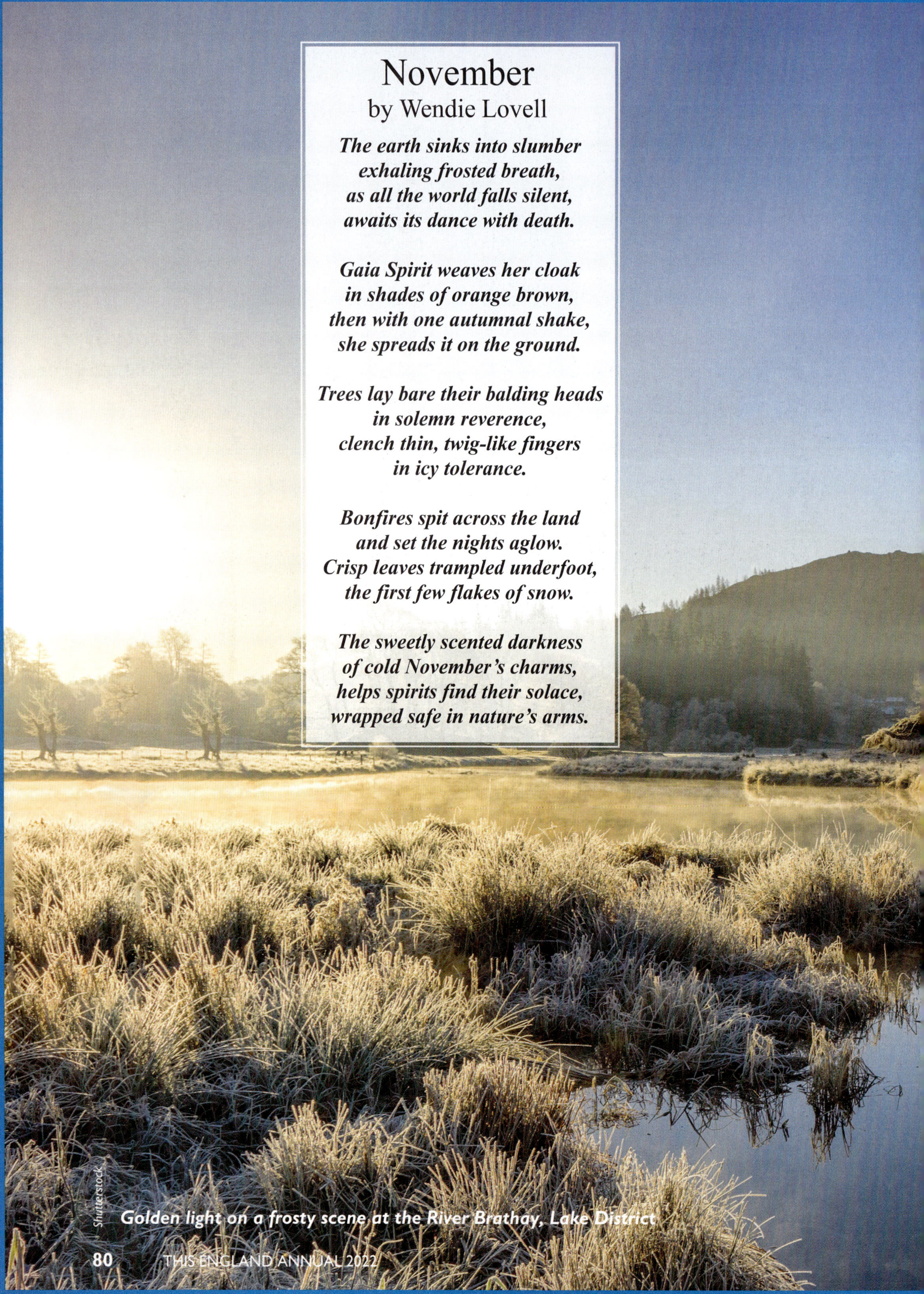

November

by Wendie Lovell

The earth sinks into slumber
exhaling frosted breath,
as all the world falls silent,
awaits its dance with death.

Gaia Spirit weaves her cloak
in shades of orange brown,
then with one autumnal shake,
she spreads it on the ground.

Trees lay bare their balding heads
in solemn reverence,
clench thin, twig-like fingers
in icy tolerance.

Bonfires spit across the land
and set the nights aglow.
Crisp leaves trampled underfoot,
the first few flakes of snow.

The sweetly scented darkness
of cold November's charms,
helps spirits find their solace,
wrapped safe in nature's arms.

Shutterstock

Golden light on a frosty scene at the River Brathay, Lake District

AUTUMN TO WINTER

Events of the season, a celebration of the Two Ronnies and a festive swim near you

AUTUMN TO WINTER

From fireworks to festive fun, Katherine Sorrell on the events of the season

OCTOBER 2022

315 YEARS AGO THIS MONTH SAW THE MEETING OF THE FIRST PARLIAMENT OF GREAT BRITAIN

The Act of Union that was passed by the English and Scottish Parliaments in 1707 led to the creation of the Kingdom of Great Britain in May of that year. And, on 23 October 1707, the Parliament of Great Britain met for the very first time at Westminster. English parliamentarians welcomed their new Scottish colleagues, but many in Scotland were unhappy at the loss of their own parliament. Their feelings were summed up by poet Robert Burns, who wrote that Scotland had "*been bought and sold for English gold*". The Scottish Parliament did not meet again until May 1999.

The House during George II's reign

SIZZLING CELEBRATIONS

All hail the great British banger! October is the month for sausage festivals. Enjoy a one-day festival in Framlingham to celebrate sausages made in East Anglia. There's another at Lincoln Castle. At both, sausage makers take over, with sizzling produce for you to try. There are food stands, live music, workshops and children's events. **framlinghamsausagefestival.com; lincolncastle.com/content/sausage-festival**

The scene of sausages

DARTMOUTH FOOD FESTIVAL

Dartmouth's Food Festival takes place towards the end of October, featuring contests, workshops, seminars, tastings and demonstrations, food and drink stalls, street entertainers and a host of fun children's activities. **dartmouthfoodfestival.com**

CHELTENHAM LITERATURE FESTIVAL

The Literature Festival at Cheltenham is one of the oldest in the world. Writers, actors, politicians and poets celebrate the joy of the written word. Visitors can take part in a ten-day programme of debates, interviews and workshops, as well as a mini festival for families. **cheltenhamfestivals.com/literature**

BFI LONDON FILM FESTIVAL

Head to the London Film Festival for a showcase of the best in contemporary world cinema – from documentaries and animation to experimental films and the latest big releases. **bfi.org.uk**

NOTTINGHAM GOOSE FAIR

This travelling fair has a history going back more than 700 years, to the days when traders would march geese to Nottingham market to be sold. Now, one of the largest funfairs in the UK, it features more than 500 attractions, from classics to new, white-knuckle experiences. **visit-nottinghamshire.co.uk/whats-on**

GREAT NORTHERN CONTEMPORARY CRAFT FAIR

The North's foremost contemporary craft fair features more than 150 designer-makers, from recent graduates to highly respected names, all selected for their excellence, showing and selling at the Victoria Baths in Hathersage, Manchester. **greatnorthernevents.co.uk**

WORLD CONKER CHAMPIONSHIPS

Held in the village of Southwick, Northamptonshire,

HORSE OF THE YEAR SHOW

Victoria Pendleton competing

Billed as the biggest week of the year for equestrian entertainment, the Horse of the Year Show, held at Birmingham's NEC, offers thrilling competitions and breathtaking displays of horsemanship, including the finals to many national showjumping championships, as well as the chance to get up close and meet some of the horses themselves. **hoys.co.uk**

on the second Sunday of October, this competition has taken place since 1965, with competitions for both adults and juniors. There's entertainment, too, and plenty of money raised for the visually impaired. **worldconkerchampionships.com**

BATTLE OF HASTINGS RE-ENACTMENT

English Heritage's biggest event of the year attracts thousands to watch armies clash on the spot in Battle, East Sussex, where King Harold and Duke William fought in 1066. See the armour worn by Saxon and Norman soldiers, meet falconers, visit the encampments for a flavour of life in an 11th-century army; or take a wander down the medieval traders' row for a souvenir. **www.english-heritage.org.uk**

TENTERDEN FOLK FESTIVAL

Taking place over four days, including the first Saturday of October, celebrating folk song, music, dance, crafts and traditions. As well as concerts and special shows, there are barn dances, sing-a-rounds, music sessions and workshops, and don't miss the procession of Morris sides and other folk dance teams on the Saturday. **tenterdenfolkfestival.org.uk**

WINTER DROVING

A Cumbrian event that harks back some 400 years to the tradition of herding animals to market. Today's event is a celebration of all things rural. The Penrith festival includes a food and craft market, street performers, live music and a torch-lit procession which features fire, drumming, giant lanterns and participants wearing animal masks. **edenarts.co.uk**

BIRMINGHAM COMEDY FESTIVAL

This ten-day, city-wide extravaganza is one of the longest-running comedy festivals in the UK. Stand-up is at its core, but you can also enjoy cabaret, improv, music, film screenings, dance performances, poetry readings and more. **bhamcomfest.co.uk**

APPLE DAY

A relatively young day of celebration, only going for a mere 32 years, 21 October features Apple Day events throughout the country. It was introduced to raise awareness of the importance of orchards and also of the provenance and traceability of food. See and try hundreds of different apples, many of them varieties not sold in regular shops; buy apple dishes and drinks, ask the "apple doctor" for advice, and identify the tree in your garden. Search local listings for events near you, or try one of the following:

- Celebrate the 2,200 varieties of apple in the national fruit collection at the National Apple Festival at Brogdale Collections, Kent. **brogdalecollections.org**
- Wander among the apple trees of Sparrow Park Orchard, Killerton, Devon, and enjoy local craft stalls, storytelling and live music. **nationaltrust.org.uk/killerton**
- Taste a wide variety of the old and new apples and pears grown at Blackmoor Estate, Hampshire, with a rural craft fair and demonstrations. It's an event that has been running for 49 years. **blackmoorestate.co.uk**
- In the walled garden at Fulham Palace, West London, the orchard will be celebrated with music, garden tours, bee keeping demonstrations, a food and crafts market, and children's activities. **fulhampalace.org**
- The Big Apple is the annual harvest time celebration of all things apple in the Herefordshire parishes of the Marcle Ridge. **bigapple.org.uk**
- Do a search for Apple Day events at sites around the country on **nationaltrust.org.uk** and at the conservation charity **ptes.org**

TRAFALGAR DAY

The most important day in the Naval calendar, Trafalgar Day commemorates Admiral Lord Nelson's victory at the Battle of Trafalgar on 21 October 1805. In Portsmouth, a ceremony takes place on board the warship *HMS Victory*, Nelson's flagship at the Battle of Trafalgar, while in London, on the closest Sunday to the 21st, hundreds of Sea Cadets demonstrate their skills and march in formation down The Mall towards Buckingham Palace – a stirring sight. **sea-cadets.org**

>

NOVEMBER 2022

LONDON TO BRIGHTON VETERAN CAR RUN

The RAC's annual extravaganza is on the first Sunday in November and sees more than 400 splendid old automobiles, all built before 1905, start in Hyde Park and (hopefully) chug all the way along the 60-mile route to a grand finish in Brighton. **veterancarrun.com**

SOMERSET CARNIVALS

Dating back to the 1600s, when many parts of the county commemorated the Gunpowder Plot, the Somerset Carnivals combine open-air entertainment, fairgrounds, street food and an incredible parade of illuminated carts that is said to be the largest in the world. They visit Somerset towns on a circuit each autumn, starting in mid-September. **scuk.co.uk**

THE WORLD'S BIGGEST LIAR

Do you enjoy telling a tall tale? Enter the competition and you'll have about five minutes to tell the biggest and most convincing lie, with no scripts or prompt cards. The prize is a much-coveted trophy, tie and beanie hat. Politicians, by the way, are considered professionals and so barred from entering. **santonbridgeinn.com/the-worlds-biggest-liar**

HAPPY 70TH BIRTHDAY TO *THE MOUSETRAP*

It's the world's longest running play, and now a legend of London's theatreland – the curtains were first raised on Agatha Christie's *The Mousetrap* at the Ambassadors Theatre on 25 November 1952. In the cast were Richard Attenborough, Sheila Sim, Martin Miller, Jessica Spencer, Aubrey Dexter, Mignon O'Doherty, Allan McClelland and John Paul. The genre-defining murder-mystery play transferred to the larger St Martin's Theatre in 1974, and went on to break every record in the history of the theatre.

The Mousetrap celebrating its 2000th performance in 1957

75 YEARS SINCE HM THE QUEEN AND THE DUKE OF EDINBURGH MARRIED

On 20 November 1947, 200 million people around the world listened to BBC Radio as the then Princess Elizabeth walked down the aisle of Westminster Abbey to marry Lieutenant Philip Mountbatten, a marriage that lasted 73 years. Two thousand guests were invited and the princess wore an ivory silk dress decorated with crystals and seed pearls, designed by Norman Hartnell, paid for using clothing ration coupons saved up by the bride. The couple received more than 2,500 wedding presents from around the world (among them a sewing machine, a fridge and a picnic case) as well as 11 wedding cakes.

The Royal Wedding, 1947

SOUTHWOLD LITERATURE FESTIVAL

Ways With Words runs a five-day literature festival in Southwold, Suffolk, a popular seaside retreat for artists and writers. Besides imbibing the literary atmosphere, you can relax with excellent wine and beers at Adnams' hotels, walk on the beach, buy fresh fish from the harbour, visit the impressive St Edmund's church, or stroll along the town's quirky pier. **wayswithwords.co.uk**

ARMISTICE DAY

At 11 am on the 11th day of the 11th month, the nation holds a two-minute silence to remember those who gave their lives in war. The National Service of Remembrance at the Cenotaph in London, attended by senior members of the Royal Family and involving a march-past of up to 10,000 veterans, is held on Remembrance Sunday, the closest Sunday to 11 November. These famous lines are from the poem *For the Fallen* by Laurence Binyon: *They shall grow not old, as we that are left grow old / Age shall not weary them, nor the years condemn / At the going down of the sun and in the morning / We will remember them.* **britishlegion.org.uk**

THE LORD MAYOR'S SHOW

The Lord Mayor's Show has its origins in King John's issue of a Royal Charter that allowed the city of London to elect its own mayor each year. The mayor travels upriver to Westminster and swears loyalty to the King. These days, marching bands, military detachments, carriages and ceremonial displays combine in the joyful procession. **lordmayorsshow.london**

AND ANOTHER 70TH BIRTHDAY – THE UK SINGLES CHART

Published by the *New Musical Express* magazine, an official list of chart-topping singles in the UK first appeared on 14 November 1952. Until then, a record's popularity had been measured by sales of its accompanying sheet music. The chart was compiled laboriously each week by *NME* founder Percy Dickins, who phoned 20 record shops around the country to ask for their biggest sales figures. The very first number one was *Here in my Heart*, by American singer Al Martino, which held on to the top spot for nine consecutive weeks.

Al Martino: first Number 1

WINTER LIGHT FESTIVALS

A growing number of dazzling light displays illuminate cities, towns and historic venues up and down the country each winter. Notable examples include those at Longleat, Kew Gardens, Canary Wharf, the National Arboretum at Westonbirt and a variety of English Heritage's historic properties. **longleat.co.uk; kew.org; canarywharf.com; forestryengland.uk; www.english-heritage.org.uk**

GUY FAWKES FESTIVAL AND FIREWORKS

This action-packed spectacular, held over a weekend in early November at the Royal Gunpowder Mills in Waltham Abbey, Essex, combines science, history, live performances, activities, food and drink, and – of course – an incredible display of fireworks. **royalgunpowdermills.com**

ST CLEMENT'S DAY BLACKSMITHS DEMONSTRATION

St Clement's Day is on 23 November and on a nearby Saturday, members of the Worshipful Company and Guild of Blacksmiths (St Clement is their patron saint) gather at Finch Foundry, near Oakhampton, Devon , to demonstrate their craft. It's the last working water-powered forge in England. **nationaltrust.org.uk/finch-foundry**

CHRISTMAS TREE THROWING

How far can you throw a six-foot Christmas tree? Enter this unusual event held each November in aid of charity at the Keele Christmas Tree Farm in Newcastle-under-Lyme, Staffordshire and find out. Entrants are judged on the height as well as length of their throws over a carefully mapped course. You know you want to! **keelechristmastreefarm.co.uk**

Choir boys of Winchester

CHRISTMAS MARKETS

Enjoy carol singing and other live entertainment, mulled wine and roasted chestnuts, fairground rides and even ice skating at Christmas markets around the country. Some are locally focused, while others aim to replicate the atmosphere of traditional continental markets. Some of the biggest include:

• Christkindelmarkt Leeds: a traditional German-style market with wooden chalet stalls, a carousel and daily programme of light entertainment. **millsqleeds.com**

• Bath Christmas Market: an award-winning market in which local makers and designers showcase their artisan gifts within 150 twinkling chalets spread out across Bath's Georgian streets. **bathchristmasmarket.co.uk**

• St Nicholas Fair, York: voted best Christmas market in the UK, it's on for six weeks across the Christmas period with live music. **visityork.org**

• Birmingham's Frankfurt Christmas Market: the biggest authentic German-style market outside Germany and Austria. There's live music and a neighbouring craft market. **thebfcm.co.uk**

• Winter Wonderland Nottingham: market stalls, entertainment, food and drink and ice skating come together at the largest event in the East Midlands. **nottinghamwinterwonderland.co.uk**

• Manchester Christmas Markets: with more than 300 beautifully festooned stalls and chalets spread across the city centre, offering international food, drink and Yuletide gifts. **visitmanchester.com**

• Winchester Cathedral Christmas Market: widely regarded as one of Europe's best, this market sees more than 100 hand-picked exhibitors offering exclusive gifts that you won't find on the high street. **winchester-cathedral.org.uk**

The Christmas market in Winchester is near the Cathedral

>

>

GRASSINGTON DICKENSIAN FESTIVAL

Transport yourself back to the time of Dickens in the picturesque village of Grassington, in the Yorkshire Dales. Over two weekends in December there'll be shopkeepers, villagers and visitors dressed in Victorian costume, accompanied by bands, buskers and Victorian-style street entertainers, plus a traditional Christmas market, a Santa's grotto and a torch-lit nativity procession.
grassingtondickensian.co.uk

It's getting Dickensian around Grassington

MONTOL

This six-day arts and community festival held in Penzance, Cornwall, celebrates the winter solstice and the county's midwinter traditions. After lantern- and mask-making workshops, carol services, storytelling, plays and late-night shopping, the festival culminates in Montol Eve on 21 December, starting with family-friendly activities during the day, and followed by an edgier, adult menu of misrule as the darkness deepens. The main draw is a lantern-lit parade through the town, with fire performers and 'Obby 'Osses, plus participants dressed in mock formal wear and masks, taking part in "Guise" dancing.
montolfestival.co.uk

Penzance's Montol Festival sees revellers take to the streets

SANTA DASH

They take place all over the country and if you can run, walk or drive a sleigh for 5k then why not join in with a fun, fancy dress "Santa dash" this December? One of the largest is at Victoria Park in the heart of East London, which transforms into a festive course for thousands – up to 4,000 – of runners dressed as Santa (and elves, reindeer, snowmen and so on) to spread Christmassy fun and raise money for charity. Places are limited, so claim yours in good time.
londonsantarun.co.uk

The Santa Dash in Victoria Park, East London

ST NICHOLAS NIGHT

Every 6 December, this community event in Alcester, Warwickshire, marks the feast day of St Nicholas, the 4th-century bishop after whom the parish church in the town of Alcester is named. As well as a parade of the Boy Bishop and attendants (played by children from the local school), town organisations and classic vehicles, there's shopping, rides, bands, Santa's grotto, Morris dancers, live music and fireworks.
alcester.co.uk

THE GREAT CHRISTMAS PUDDING RACE

A unique event taking place on the cobbles around London's Covent Garden, where teams in fancy dress compete (on behalf of the charity Cancer Research UK) to complete a festive course – while balancing a Christmas pudding on a tray. Not an easy task . . .
xmaspuddingrace.org.uk

TREE DRESSING

Tree Dressing is based on many old customs from all over the world and takes place during National Tree Week on the first weekend in December. Communities right across the UK come together and celebrate by "dressing" a tree in ribbons, bunting or other decorations.
commonground.org.uk/tree-dressing-day

WINTER WATCH AND SATURNALIA PARADE

This midwinter spectacle on the streets of Chester features a re-enactment of the Winter Watch, a ceremony dating from the 15th century, when the good burghers would put the keys to the city in the safe hands of an early version of the local police force. The party really starts when the Lord of Misrule and a mischievous gathering of fire breathers, devils, skeletons, ice queens, Jack Frosts and even bloodthirsty cooks (bearing a head on a platter), dance around the city centre to the relentless beating of drums, with an amazing finale of firebreathing. **midsummerwatch.co.uk/winter-watch-parade**

BOXING DAY "SQUIRT"

The volunteer fire brigade in Geddington, Northamptonshire, are behind this annual Boxing Day "Squirt" – essentially a water fight against a friendly local fire-station rival – in which a beer barrel is suspended from a rope over the local river and the two teams attempt to push the barrel over the heads of their opposition using their hose jets. Visitors are advised to wear waterproof clothing! **gvfb.org/squirt**

TOM BAWCOCK'S EVE

On the day before Christmas Eve villagers in Cornwall's picturesque Mousehole celebrate the heroic efforts of legendary Tom Bawcock, who is said to have alleviated a famine by going out to fish in a severe storm. Watch the lantern procession, enjoy the village's famous display of lights, then head to the Ship Inn and you'll be served a slice of "stargazy pie" – a fish pie with the heads sticking out of the pastry. The custom was the inspiration behind Antonia Barber's famous children's book *The Mousehole Cat*. **shipinnmousehole.co.uk**

TAR BAR'L

A New Year's Eve fire festival in the town of Allendale, Northumberland, that is thought to date as far back as the Middle Ages, but has certainly been celebrated for at least 160 years as a way of seeing out the old year and welcoming in the new. The focal point of the night of music and dancing is a procession of 45 local men who wear colourful fancy dress and carry whisky barrels filled with burning tar. At midnight they light a ceremonial bonfire, as everyone shouts, "Be damned to he who throws last!" **visitnorthumberland.com**

NEW YEAR'S EVE FIREWORKS

They'll be happening all over the country, but the biggest event is in the capital, where the UK's largest annual fireworks display takes place over the London Eye reflected in the Thames to the accompaniment of Big Ben's "bongs". Having been cancelled to the public at the end of 2020, it will be good to see them back in both 2021 and 2022. Bear in mind that if you want to brave the crowds, you'll need a ticket to attend. If not, they're usually shown on TV. **london.gov.uk**

MATLOCK BATH RAFT EVENT

A Boxing Day "race" to raise money for the RNLI. Fearless, water-loving and slightly bonkers entrants from all over the country float decorated rafts down the River Derwent from Cawdor Quarry in Matlock to Cromford Meadows, watched by a huge turnout of spectators. **matlockraftevent.co.uk**

Charity rafting on Boxing Day near Matlock

THE 70TH ANNIVERSARY OF THE "GREAT SMOG"

5 December 1952: the city of London is brought to an almost complete standstill by a lethal fog, the result of a combination of industrial pollution and high-pressure weather conditions. The "great smog" lasted for five days and caused around 12,000 deaths. Polluted fogs had been a feature of the capital for centuries (King James I had tried, ineffectively, to restrict the burning of coal in the 1600s); they became known as "pea soupers" because of their yellow and dense appearance. The 1952 fog, however, was the worst ever. Ambulances were unable to get around, cars were abandoned on the roads and even indoor plays had to be stopped because the audiences could not see the stage. Four years later, the Government passed the Clean Air Act in direct response, now considered a major advance in both public health and the history of environmental action.

Mist at a Hyde Park gate

Day-time during the smog

Images: Shutterstock, Alamy

ENGLISH BRIDGES

IRON, SHROPSHIRE

Isobel King reflects on an icon of the Industrial Revolution

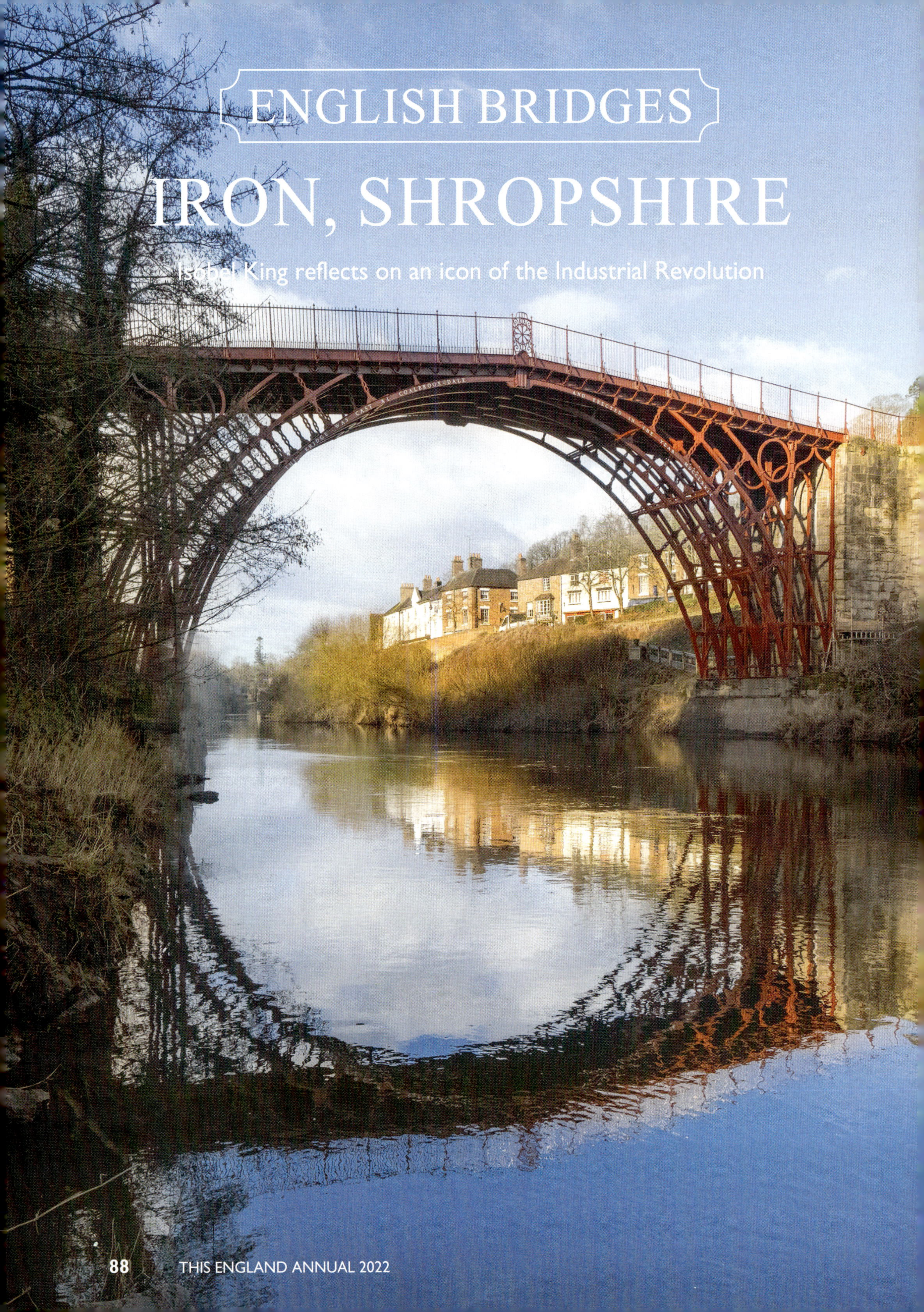

A blacksmith at work, Blists Hill

Stunning tiles at Jackfield

Coalport's bottle kilns

"IT is one arch, a hundred feet broad, fifty-two high, and eighteen wide; all of cast-iron, weighing many hundred tons. I doubt whether the Colossus at Rhodes weighed much more," said cleric John Wesley of the world's first metal bridge.

That bronze titan, Colossus, reputedly 110 feet tall, stood for only 50 years before being toppled by an earthquake. The Iron Bridge stands more than 240 years later, formally opened on New Year's Day 1781 – its might seeing off the Great Flood back in 1795 right up to the recent flooding of 2020. It's been an Ancient Monument in its own right since 1934.

A lasting symbol of the Industrial Revolution, the bridge stands in UNESCO's Ironbridge Gorge. It was in this stunning valley, shaped during the Ice Age, and the 550 surrounding hectares, that the revolution started and spread, causing some of the most far-reaching changes in human history. Home to the raw materials that transformed industrial processes, mines were dug, factories, foundries and warehouses built, and river and road transport developed. Artists, writers and engineers were drawn here from far and wide. It remains a world-famous place to visit.

A mile away in Coalbrookdale, in 1709, Abraham Darby first smelted iron using coke to fuel furnaces instead of charcoal. It made mass production of cast iron financially viable, a key breakthrough in getting the wheels of revolution turning. Iron trade in Britain boomed. Continuing the dynasty of iron masters, the Iron Bridge itself was built by his grandson Abraham Darby III. With such a name involved, it's easy to overlook that the bridge was actually designed by Thomas Farnolls Pritchard, with Darby only overseeing the project after Pritchard's death in 1777.

Since 1934, the bridge has been closed to traffic so today you can stroll across in our nation's historic footsteps. An exhibition in the original Tollhouse explains how and why it was built. You can hire kayaks, too, paddling alongside kingfishers, wagtails and swans, enjoying the bridge from the river.

For me, Iron Bridge is as much a reminder of family as a symbol of industry. My father's happiest childhood memories were forged in this town, staying with a dear aunt and uncle in one of the houses that still cling to the sides of the beautiful Gorge. Their home had no electricity, lit by Tilley lamps, but such was its magic he'd count down the days to visiting. It's what brought him back to Shropshire later in life making the town part of my past and that of my six siblings – the Iron Bridge a backdrop to many of our fledgling recriminations and reconciliations.

And it's still there. Grown in beauty even since those industrial days when it was likely engulfed by belches of smoke. The scene is lovely year round from summer's lush green to the framing of an auburn autumn. There was an austereness about it in winter, all white frost on grey, but in 2017 it was painted in its original red-brown. Now it radiates a festive warmth, mirrored by the flowing river below.

THINGS TO DO IN IRONBRIDGE

Blists Hill Victorian Town

Find a cure for drunkenness in the chemist, talk about the "latest" Parisian fashions at the drapers, and visit the bank to exchange modern money for old-fashioned currency to spend in the shops and pubs of this open-air living museum.

Madeley, Nr Ironbridge, Telford TF7 5DU; 01952 433424

Jackfield Tile Museum

Gas-lit galleries and period room settings show off dazzling tiles all made in what was once the heart of British tile production. The museum is housed in the UK's best surviving example of a Victorian tile factory and you can still see artists at work. Jackfield was important to navigation, coal mining and clay production.

Jackfield, Ironbridge TF8 7LJ; 01952 433424

Coalport China Musuem

Coalport was one of the country's largest porcelain manufacturers, with a global reputation for fine china. Its treasures were sought after by the wealthy and even royalty. See traditional techniques in the riverside workshops and step inside the atmospheric kilns.

High Street, Telford TF8 7HT; 01952 580650

All are run by the Ironbridge Gorge Museums Trust: ironbridge.org.uk

Images: Alamy, Shutterstock, Ironbridge Gorge Museums Trust

"AND IT'S *Goodnight* FROM HIM"

Amanda Hodges pays tribute to the Two Ronnies, whose shows and Christmas specials were a firm fixture in the nation's calendar

The dynamic duo in the 1970s

JULY 2005, and *The Two Ronnies Christmas Sketchbook* was being recorded months ahead of transmission, its date accelerated by the fragile state of Ronnie Barker's health. Decades since their 1971 debut, the programme was genially reviewing classic sketches, introducing a new generation to their distinctive brand of comedy. The beloved catchphrase adopted to end their weekly show conjured images of the duo at their effervescent best, yet now held added poignancy.

The Christmas 1987 show had been momentous for it was at this juncture that Ronnie Barker effectively retired from the rigours of filming *The Two Ronnies*, confiding in Ronnie Corbett a year earlier that, aged only fifty-eight he was pausing, seeking a quieter pace of life, "to stop and smell the roses" as former boss Michael Grade aptly termed it.

Their festive shows had become an established part of the nation's Christmas celebrations and their seasonal special was considered the jewel in the BBC's festive crown. In general though, they had enjoyed 16 years at the top in this show, a beloved television fixture, Ronnie Hazelhurst's opening music with the signature image of two pairs of glasses signalling the start of an entertaining Saturday evening. Their blend of zany news items, silly sketches and spoof monologues had 19 million watching at its zenith.

"Part of the magic of *The Two Ronnies* was the atmosphere, somehow it percolated into TV sets at home," Barker said.

But how did *The Two Ronnies* come into being? Their rise to primetime prominence hinged on an unlikely premise, namely their verbal dexterity at a London Palladium BAFTA evening when a technical hitch led to an eight minute improvisation, done with such consummate skill that Bill Cotton, Head of Light Entertainment, was duly impressed. The pair were offered their own primetime show shortly afterwards.

The story of how they first met could have come straight out of a sketch. In 1963 Corbett was working as a barman, in between jobs, at the Buckstone Club in

London, a regular actors' haunt. Barker frequented the place and in his own memoir recalled, "A voice came out of thin air and I thought it was the drink talking until something made me peer over the other side of the bar and there he was!"

In time the story expanded, with Corbett purportedly standing on boxes marked *Champ* and *Agnes*, ("Champagne"!) but Corbett always denied this as fabrication, saying he was perfectly visible.

A few years later David Frost chose them for his 1966 pioneering programme, *The Frost Report*. Here they cemented their friendship, as Corbett recalls in his autobiography: "Ronnie and I got on well from the start. There was immediate comfort between us. . . a sensible reserve in our relationship. It was, if you like, the beginning of a very British friendship."

Each programme embraced a different subject, Frost giving a spoof monologue and a supporting cast performing various skits. Witness early signs of Corbett's immaculate comic timing in the delightful "Do Not Walk On The Grass" sketch where he, bowler-hatted, ingeniously thwarts police scrutiny by crossing the grass in every fashion – save that of actually walking!

So by the time Corbett and Barker came to star on *The Two Ronnies* they knew each other, and each other's comedic style, well. The larger, more rotund Barker was essentially a character actor of infinite versatility, the diminutive Corbett a gifted vaudevillian. Barker found his niche playing an impressive variety of characters from country yokels to peers, whilst Corbett's innate comic ability found expression both in sketches and solo shaggy dog monologues.

Both men hailed from similar backgrounds, grammar-school boys who realised their calling early in life, Corbett from Edinburgh, Barker from Oxford. Corbett eschewed further education after amateur theatricals

During filming at Lulworth Cove, Dorset

convinced him of his destiny. "I knew I wanted to be an actor . . . a comic actor."

He did his National Service with the Royal Air Force and was, at only five feet tall, the shortest commissioned officer in the British Forces! After what he called eight "lean years" where he'd worked whilst "resting" as a caretaker and managed tennis court reservations, he inched towards the limelight, yet "never doubted what I wanted to do and there was never any question of giving up."

Barker found success earlier, after stints working in architecture and a bank. He joined Manchester repertory theatre company, perfecting his craft there and in the West End, probably gaining the rich feeling for the English language that served him so well on *The Two Ronnies* where his delight in wordplay was palpable. Getting a laugh was similarly pivotal for him early on.

"The thrill that I experienced on hearing that most wonderful of sounds . . .This is what I want to do, I thought. Never mind Hamlet . . . Give me Charley's Aunt!"

Although Barker was acclaimed by Sir Peter Hall as " the great (dramatic) actor we never had," (latterly playing character roles in *The Gathering Storm* and *My House in Umbria*,) Corbett himself felt that Barker had found his true

MASTERMIND

One of the duo's best-loved skits almost never happened. "Having sat down and written the sketch, I tore it up," admits writer David Renwick. "The following day, because I'd no better ideas and had to deliver something, I literally fished the pieces out of the waste bin."

Thank goodness he did. First broadcast 1 November 1980 on the BBC, the skit shows just how topical *The Two Ronnies* could be: poking fun at the warring then General Secretary of the TUC, Len Murray, and Chancellor of the Exchequer Geoffrey Howe, it's done with such surreal silliness, everyone was momentarily brought together even across such a vast political divide . . .

Magnus: And so to our first contender. Good evening and can I have your name, please?
Charlie Smithers: Ah . . . good evening.
Magnus: Your chosen subject was answering questions before they were asked. This time you have chosen to answer the question before last, correct?
Charlie Smithers: Charlie Smithers.
Magnus: And your time starts now. What is palaeontology?
Charlie Smithers: Yes, absolutely correct.
Magnus: What is the name of the directory that lists members of the peerage?
Charlie Smithers: A study of old fossils.
Magnus: Correct. Who are Len Murray and Sir Geoffrey Howe?
Charlie Smithers: Burke's.
Magnus: What is the difference between a donkey and an ass?
Charlie Smithers: One's a trade union leader, the other's a member of the Cabinet.

>

NEWS BRIEFING

Is there any other more recognisable image of *The Two Ronnies* than at their news desk? Barker's witty wordplay, evinced in his one-liners (such as these two below), garnered legions of fans thanks to being a style of humour the whole family could share in.

A cement mixer has collided with a prison van. Motorists are asked to look out for 16 hardened criminals.

A vicar who rode his bike the wrong way up the M1 was asked how he managed to avoid an accident. He replied "God was with me" and was furthered charged for riding two on a bike.

metier. "He always believed that comedy was as important as serious work, and that making millions laugh on television was just as good as moving smaller numbers of people to tears in the theatre." Barker agreed. "There's something special about comedy, an extra spark . . .
I wouldn't have dreamed of doing anything else."

Interestingly, neither wished to embrace traditional territory. "We weren't a double act, just two friends and solo performers who happened to do one series in partnership," Barker affirmed. Both maintained separate careers, Corbett scoring success with *Sorry!* and Barker appearing in "the best work I ever did"; the inimitable and much-loved *Porridge*.

Aware of potential gags likely because of his stature, Corbett felt a traditional set-up would see him the inevitable butt of physical comedy and wanted to sidestep this. Although his height is often mentioned he's rarely the conventional stooge, the men occupy equal comedic footing. Corbett also revealed that the intensely private Barker felt happiest in character and never liked to talk directly to an audience; such hesitancy lay behind the evolution of their "goodnight" catchphrase as it gave a clear framework within which Barker felt comfortable.

But there was no name for the embryonic show. Despite being labelled "the two Ronnies" during *The Frost Report* it wasn't until someone formally suggested the name that they realised just how apposite it was. As a vehicle the show was perfect for them, both men disciplined performers and, as Corbett emphasised, "we were well prepared, theatrically experienced and thoughtful . . . attention to detail was our watchword."

Spoof news items were staged as newsreaders, the two men sitting side by side to begin and end the show. Guest acts diminished over time (unless it was their own long-haired country and western duo Jehosaphat and Jones) but they knew variety of pace was pivotal so always combined regular sketches (party ones a speciality) with filmed material like serials *The Phantom Raspberry Blower of Old London Town* (written by Spike Milligan and Barker) or hapless detective pair Piggy Malone (always scoffing) and boyish sidekick Charley Farley.

"It was a good format because although the same every week it allowed scope for enormous variety in the jokes within that format. It combined familiarity with freshness," Corbett felt.

To say these sketches were eclectic is an understatement; their appeal remains timeless. From the daft delights of Corbett's racing pigeon – which is actually a duck – to the exasperation of Barker's shopkeeper with the sweetshop customer from hell, they mined such a rich seam of material, delivered so impeccably, that their best work has truly stood the test of time. Each Ronnie had his own distinctive moment too, Barker always first, in character, with something like the gloriously garbled *Pismonouncers Unanimous* and Corbett's discursive chair monologues ending in more leisurely fashion.

Michael Palin said of the pair, "they were very different in the way they performed and the characters they could play, but complemented each other well.

Barker with Fulton Mackay in Porridge, 1979

Cast and writers from The Frost Report, 1967 (Barker is front right)

Corbett fooling around as Timothy Lumsden in Sorry! 1986

Both were supreme deliverers of a funny line."

Unlike Barker who admitted innate perfectionism and enjoyed writing material, Corbett was happy to leave the scripts to others and in due course the likes of David Nobbs (*The Fall and Rise of Reginald Perrin*), David Renwick (*One Foot in the Grave*), Michael Palin, and one Gerald Wiley (Barker himself under a pseudonym) all contributed.

"Ronnie Barker was essentially an actor who learned how to make people laugh. Ronnie Corbett adapted his own very physical skills to master the art of acting," said Renwick.

"Barker's trick, like Sellers and Guinness, was to disappear into a multitude of identities. Corbett was always recognisably himself, investing every role with the same trademark twinkle."

Amazingly, despite their long association, the pair never argued or fell out. Corbett said, "trust was the cornerstone of our relationship," as Barker endorsed, "We were very similar as people . . . The main factor in *The Two Ronnies'* success is that we're on the same comedy wavelength." Any sketch not given joint approval was rejected.

"We struck a balance. If I'd most of the funny lines in one sketch, Ronnie got plenty in the next. That brought constant variety within the format of what became a bit of an institution."

As the show entered the Eighties it was parodied unfairly on *Not The Nine O'Clock News*, and derided amidst the new landscape of alternative comedy.

"In this harsh world there are worse things to be than cosy," said Corbett, their show "a moment for the whole family to sit and relax together without embarrassment."

He added, "Comedians these days forget they are in people's living-rooms. That requires good manners. It is possible to have good manners and be funny at the same time. Ronnie Barker and I proved that."

Yes, there were naughty double entendres galore (courtesy of Barker's love of seaside postcards) but, as Barker declared, "I think we offered the most acceptable form of general comedy, something to amuse most people without upsetting or insulting them."

The best testament to the quality of their material and their comedic legacy is the affection in which the duo are still held; none other than Robbie Williams has paid homage to their inspiration by having their signature glasses tattooed on his neck. Eight million viewers watched the rebooted *Sketchbook* in the early Noughties.

"It was forty years of harmonious joy, nothing but an absolute pleasure," said Corbett of his association with Barker – a friendship that brought us, as the audience, abundant joy, too.

They're not new but The Two Ronnies *autobiographies still make a cracking read.* It's Hello from Him, *Ronnie Barker (New English Library); And it's* Goodnight from Him, *Ronnie Corbett with David Nobbs (Penguin).*

PISMONUNCERS UNANIMOUS

Displaying another facet of Ronnie Barker's verbal dexterity and love of spoonerisms, this is one of his solo sketches which amply displays what Ronnie Corbett praised as his "great mastery of the English language."

Good evening. I am the president for the loyal society for the relief of sufferers from pismonunciation; for people who cannot say their worms correctly. Or who use the wrong worms entirely, so that other people cannot underhand a bird they are spraying . . .

Images: Shutterstock

Swimmers don tinsel and santa hats for the Serpentine Christmas Day Swim

TAKE THE PLUNGE

Imogen Bole is here to tempt you to ten of the very best festive swims

IT'S widely accepted that England's long festive tradition of delving into nippy waters was first established by the founders of the Brighton Swimming Club. In 1858, a small group of North Street tradesmen gathered on Albion Beach and took to the waters simply to learn how to swim. So successful were their endeavours that they introduced "marine antics", comprising, amongst other larks, the exchanging of two fully dressed swimmers' clothes and floating tea parties! The club, founded in 1860, continued to host the annual dip.

When, in 1864, the high-profile Serpentine Swimming Club hosted their first Christmas swim, the chilly custom captured the attention of the capital. Since the 1860s, countless festive swims have sprouted up across England and grown exponentially in their popularity, with many still tempting hardy swimmers today.

Below, you'll find a mere portion of the legacy left behind by those North Street tradesmen, spanning the length and breadth of the country and the English Channel. These beautiful settings, historic venues and rallying atmospheres might just convince you to try.

And if not? Well, you can always make a donation and have a jolly chortle on the sidelines!

The Weymouth Harbour Christmas Day Swim

With the multicoloured Georgian and Victorian townhouses, so typical of the English seaside town as your backdrop, why not brave the bracing waters at Weymouth Harbour?

The traditional Christmas Day swim started as a late-night (post-pub) dip by locals Dill and Reggie in 1948. And it has been organised by the Weymouth Portland Lions Club since the mid-1970s, with the number and bravery of its participants growing each year. The objective is to dive in from the wooden deck beneath the promenade at one side of the harbour and swim to the other. It may not be for the faint-hearted, but it's for some worthy causes.

Mark Lockie of the Weymouth & Portland Lions Club says of the event, "Swimmers come from all over the country to take part, and many just turn up on the day. The amount of money raised each year for local and national charities is in the region of £20,000." *10:30am, £10; weymouthlionsclub.co.uk*

Clevedon Marine Lake's New Year's Day Dip

In its heyday, Clevedon Marine

Lake was a hugely popular seaside attraction, built in 1929, just eight miles up the coast from Weston-super-Mare. Equipped with a timber clubhouse and changing room, high diving and springboards, a bathing raft, deckchairs, a row of bathing huts and a bandstand, it's hardly surprising the resort held such appeal. That is, until the 1970s when visitor numbers declined in favour of foreign travel.

In 2004, the Marlens charity was established to revive Clevedon after its years of neglect. The charity's work saw sailing, canoeing, open-water swimming and model boat sailing return to Clevedon. An additional £800,000 from the Heritage Lottery Fund returned Clevedon to its bygone splendour.

The first festive swim was then held on New Year's Day in 2016. Swimmers would dress up as Edwardians and take to Clevedon beaches at high tide. A Boxing Day dip has since been added.

So, if after all the hectic Christmas plans, you want some simple serenity by Salthouse Bay, Clevedon's the swim for you. *11am, Free; clevedonmarinelake.co.uk*

Serpentine Christmas Day Swim

Swimmers have gathered in London's Hyde Park on Christmas morning since 1864 to take part in the historic swim in the Serpentine.

Each competitor has their eye on the Peter Pan Cup, donated to the Serpentine Club in 1904 by J.M. Barrie himself, who presented it to the winner each year until 1932.

Women couldn't join until 1930, and began receiving their own separate trophy in the 1990s. The inferior Wendy Cup was awarded to the first woman home, but after a swimmer named Emmi Hunte won the entire race and was presented with the much smaller trophy, a long overdue motion was carried in 2005 to award the Peter Pan Cup to the winner, irrespective of gender.

The Serpentine race is only open to club members who have swum earlier in the season. This not only allows the handicaps to be calculated, but it prepares competitors for the race that is swum without wetsuits in temperatures usually below 5°C. *9am, annual membership fee £20, Christmas race free for members; serpentineswimmingclub.com*

Saltdean Lido's Christmas Day Swim

A lido where watching Jay Gatsby take a reviving dip wouldn't seem out of sorts, Brighton's Saltdean was built in the style of contemporary ocean liners in 1938. The Thirties was the decade dubbed "the golden age of lidos", when sybaritic escapes could be found on home turf, until overseas travel became more affordable.

Having enjoyed just two summer seasons, Saltdean was forced to close in 1940 at the outbreak of World War II. Playing its own part in the war effort, the Streamline Moderne-style lido was requisitioned by the Auxiliary Fire Service, who used the pool as a water tank and the grounds to conduct training exercises.

This temple to outdoor swimming has been restored to its roaring '30s glory days, so much so that in 2015, Historic England named Saltdean as one of England's "seven seaside wonders".

As of 2018, the Grade II listed lido began hosting a Christmas Day swim, when more than 150 Santa-hatted swimmers took to the heated waters. *8am & 9am, £10; saltdeanlido.org*

Sunderland's Boxing Day Dip

Should you find yourself wandering along the Seaburn promenade at 11am on Boxing Day, you certainly won't be walking alone. You may, however, be the only one not in fancy dress.

Around a thousand brave souls will be charging towards the North Sea from the Grand Hotel's changing rooms to raise money for a host of worthy causes both in the UK and abroad.

Originating in 1975 as a small charity event for members of the Sunderland Lions Club, the Boxing Day Dip is one of the older festive swims of its kind, which over the years has swelled to be one of the largest Boxing Day swims in Europe, even drawing swimmers from the warmer waters of Australia and New Zealand.

If it's tradition, a beautiful stretch of sand and a spirited crowd you're after, look no further. And go the extra mile with your costume: there's a prize for best-dressed! *11am, £25; e-clubhouse.org/sites/sunderland_uk*

Stunning skies at Clevedon

A brave line up in Hyde Park!

Could that be our PM?

"It's cold!" The faces say it all at Clevedon Marine Lake

Crowds turn out for St Elizabeth Hospice in Felixstowe

Hathersage Lido's Carol Concert

Innocuously nestled in the Derbyshire Dales, within the Peak District National Park, Hathersage Lido sits on the valley slope of the River Derwent, on the eastern edge of the Hope Valley. Should you visit in late December, you could be swimming to the sound of your favourite carols.

Built in 1936, thanks to a generous donation by local philanthropist and industrialist George H. Lawrence, the lido boasted a bandstand with 236 chairs, two all-weather tennis courts, a large paddling pool, a sand pit, a gymnasium, a refreshment room, a sunbathing parlour of Vita glass and gardens. Historical photos of Hathersage show just how popular the lido was with everyone, from honeymooning couples to the local Sheffield United Football team.

Just four years after its construction, Hathersage's benefactor was tragically killed, as were many of his workers, in his Sheffield factory when it suffered a direct hit during a German air raid. *18 Dec, 12pm (carols). 24 Dec & 1 Jan (festive swims), various times, £7 (adult), £4 (child). hathersageswimmingpool.co.uk*

Blackroot Pool's Christmas Day Plunge

Blackroot Pool, located in the 2,400-acre Sutton Park National Nature Reserve near Sutton Coldfield, was built in the 18th century for the express purpose of powering a watermill. Originally known as Perkin's Pool, Blackroot is thought to have acquired its current name from the blackened stump of an old oak tree near the centre of the pool.

Submerging yourself in one of Sutton Park's seven historic pools is to immerse yourself in centuries of history, with some lakes dating back to the medieval period, and the surrounding grounds once forming a 12th-century deer park.

Swimmers have been braving the Sutton Park lakes since 1899, when swimming galas, known as "Water Carnivals", were first hosted by the Boldmere Swimming Club in Powell's Pool. And it was in Blackroot Pool where the first annual Christmas Day swim was held by the Winter Swimming Club. *10am, Free*

Otley's New Year's Day Swim

Since 2011, the Yorkshire market town's New Year's Day Swim in the river Wharfe has been known to locals as the Joe Town Memorial Swim in memory of the lifesaving swimming teacher who had run the swim for 25 years.

Joe Town started the swim in the mid-1980s, and took part every year up to 2009. There was one year that he missed at the age of 83 when the river was frozen.

Joe's daughter, Helen, said: "I am glad to say it is still going, and the event is getting bigger and bigger each year. In 2011, about twenty-five people did the swim, and my dad cried with joy. He had hoped the swim would go on for years and years."

Tens of hardy swimmers now brace themselves along the 20-metre stretch of river by the Wharfemeadows Park at noon before lowering themselves into the fortifying waters, all in the name of charity. In 2020, 91 swimmers took part – the youngest nine years old and the oldest seventy-one. *12pm, Free*

Felixstowe's Christmas and New Year's Day Dips

The Suffolk seaside town's Christmas Day Dip first began in the early 2000s as a challenge set by local resident Peter Burt in a private pool. When passers-by wanted to contribute, Peter donated the money to the independent Suffolk charity, St Elizabeth Hospice, where his father was later cared for.

The popularity of the swim grew to such an extent that Peter handed over the reins to the hospice, who took the swim to the sea and added a New Year's Day Dip to the Felixstowe calendar.

Joanne Rodger, events and challenges manager at the hospice, said: "The hospice's Christmas Day Dip has the most incredible community atmosphere, where people come together on Christmas Day morning to support each other taking on the chilly challenge.

"The event normally raises around an amazing £40,000 each year. For some people, the Christmas Day Dip has become a family tradition, to take part or to spectate." *10am on both days, £5 (participants are asked to raise sponsorship); stelizabethhospice.org.uk*

La Vallette's tidal pools, Guernsey

The Polar Bear Swim at La Vallette Bathing Pools, Guernsey

If you fancy venturing further afield, leaving English shores for the Bailiwick of Guernsey in the English Channel, you'll be greeted by La Vallette's four magnificent coastal swimming pools.

Perfectly positioned under the Havelet Bay cliffs, these pools are a stalwart example of the ingenuity of Victorian engineering. They are flushed twice a day at high tide, and their high walls filter out seaweed and sea creatures.

The Horseshoe pool was built first in 1844 and offers panoramic views over Guernsey's neighbouring islands.

Such was the beauty of this particular marine gem that it attracted the likes of Victor Hugo, who spent 15 years on the island while in exile from France between 1855 and 1870, during which time he penned his greatest work, *Les Misérables*.

The traditional swim has been run on the morning of Christmas Day by the Guernsey Swimming Club for over 100 years, except during the German occupation of the Channel Islands from 1940-1945. *9:30am, Free. guernseyswimming.com*

These swims are undoubtedly some of the best-loved events in the country's communal swimming calendar, but safety must always come first. Please do visit the Outdoor Swimming Society's website for their top tips on staying safe before diving in at outdoorswimmingsociety.com.

CHARITABLY CHILLY

What may ease the dread of hurling yourself into some pretty low temperatures is knowing it's all in the name of some extremely worthy causes.

There are a number of historic outdoor swimming venues, which at some point in their history fell into disrepair. Thankfully, there's been a considerable push to restore pools like Saltdean, Hathersage and Clevedon Marine Lake. The funds raised from the festive swims at these locations contribute to the continued efforts to preserve these slices of swimming history for generations to come.

Both the Weymouth Harbour Christmas Day Swim and the Sunderland Boxing Day Dip are run by their local Lions Club, a network of charitable bodies providing financial support to local causes and overseas appeals, ranging from local foodbanks and football clubs to Help for Heroes and the Australian bushfires.

The Felixstowe swim raises money solely for the local St Elizabeth Hospice, which works to improve the lives of its 3,000 patients living with a progressive illness and life-limiting conditions, as well as supporting family members suffering a bereavement.

Admission to the Serpentine's Christmas swim is free for members. However, you must be a member to take part, and upon signing up, swimmers are given the option of making a donation to the Level Water charity, which provides specialist one-to-one swimming lessons for children with physical and sensory disabilities. This financial year, the Serpentine has donated £13,573 to the charity.

Some festive swims leave the choice of charity to the swimmers. Participants of Blackroot Pool's Christmas swim fundraise independently, as it's no longer an officially organised event. And positioned along the River Wharfe are bucket collections for local and national charities, chosen by the swimmers for the work they do. Those causes have included Sands, a stillbirth and neonatal death charity, and Camphill Village Trust, which supports adults with learning disabilities, autism and mental health challenges.

A standout team effort at Weymouth Harbour

Images: Shutterstock, Alamy, St Elizabeth Hospice, Guernsey Swimming Club, Serpentine Swimming Club, Weymouth & Portland Lions Club, Rowan Clarke

David on a well-earned break

A LONDON JOURNEY

It's 125 years since the first mechanically propelled cab took to London's streets. Cabbie David Styles drives us back in time

IT'S 10.30 on a winter's night and, stopping at a set of traffic lights, I can just recognise a familiar face approaching through the falling snow. It is Jeremy Clarkson making his way towards my cab's warm interior.

"Sorry, Jeremy. I'm booked," I have to inform him.

I pulled away to pick up my fare – actor Bill Nighy – who took delight at being given priority! In all my years as a cabbie, I've been lucky to have had so many famous faces in the back seat.

Once, though, the inside of a cab didn't offer a refuge – far from it. Hansom carriages, pulled by a horse, were open to the elements for the cabbie and gave scant protection for his passenger. Then, 125 years ago in 1897, Walter Bersey introduced to London his electric cabs.

Affectionately known by cabbies as "'Ummingbirds" because of the sound they made, they had batteries strapped under the body and could travel for 30 miles at a maximum speed of nine mph! The Bersey was almost certainly the first mechanically propelled cab in the world and, like their famous predecessor, today's latest cabs are now also propelled by electricity.

My first cab, some 26 years ago, also had little protection from the elements. It was the "classic" that could have featured in a post-war film with Cary Grant hailing it on a rain-swept London street.

The designers of this Austin FX4 taxi incorporated some novel features. It had a steering wheel so large it wouldn't have looked out of place on an ocean liner. It also had the startling habit of swerving wildly just as you approached a narrow road restriction.

Its heating was continually activated. A clever piece of British technology ensured that hot water from the engine could bypass a valve meant to arrest the flow, and couldn't be turned off. In contrast, the windscreen wipers were wholly ineffective.

The FX4 may have been engineering at its zenith when designed, but the vehicles were still in production 50 years later. It made them considerably more enduring than Walter Bersey's prodigy: his vehicles stayed in service for only two years.

Another concession for the FX4 to 20th-century motoring was a radio. I suppose passengers were complaining to the Public Carriage Office about cabbies talking too much. Today 24-hour Talk Sport radio broadcasting has relieved many passengers from listening to their driver's opinion of the shortcomings of England's manager.

Driving a London cab has its compensations: how many people spend their workday with an ever-changing view from their office? Who gets to start and go home when they fancy without disciplinary action? Who's visited Downing Street, the American Ambassador's residence, or Buckingham Palace, while talking, as I have done, to John Hurt, Martin Clunes or David Walliams?

London cabbies are a band of over 20,000 professionals who know everything there is to know about the city – a conurbation with so many theatres that you could, if you had the time, go to a different production every single day for the rest of your life and never see the same show twice.

There's only one problem with the capital's black cab drivers: we are the best and we're determined to let everyone know about it!

This all-encompassing, irrefutable superiority comes down to one simple and also very complicated concept: The Knowledge. This series of tests, which must be passed in order to obtain your cabbie's licence, requires the memorisation of 320 routes, 25,000 roads and the thousands of points of interest all over London. To get a passenger from one place to another by the shortest route, you need to know the city like the back of your hand.

It took me four years, 10 months and 13 days to conquer it, studying over 30 hours a week, while holding down a full-time job and

Driving amid Regent Street's Christmas lights . . .

A 1958 Austin FX3 taxi

travelling over 20,000 miles. The Knowledge is an undertaking thousands have tried, but only a small proportion accomplish.

Why is the casualty rate so enormous? For one thing, London is the most unplanned big city in the world. Even rebuilding after the Great Fire produced no handy grids, or grand avenues similar to Paris or New York. All we have is a complex arrangement of random roads, streets, squares, parks and the odd cul-de-sac. If it weren't for the Blitz, that unsanctioned bit of urban renewal initiated by Hitler, sections of the City of London would be an even bigger labyrinth of cabbie-confounding alleys.

Despite Adolf's efforts, London is full of delightful idiosyncrasies. For instance, the Circle Line is not circular. Queensway Station is in Bayswater, while Bayswater Station is found in, you guessed it, Queensway. Harrods isn't in the road named Knightsbridge and the immoveable Greenwich Meridian Line has moved.

The oddness that London is imbued with also stretches to its cabbies. The respected Labour Member of Parliament, Tony Benn, seemed to understand the London cab trade better than most. As a regular passenger, he would strike up a conversation with the driver, asking: "And what did you do before becoming a cabbie?"

London's cabbies come from a diverse array of occupations. There are builders, musicians, teachers and members of the emergency services and, in past times, many were recruited from London's docks and newspapers. Jews fleeing persecution once joined the ranks in large numbers, some Yiddish having entered the cabbies' lexicon. Derived from public carriages used in Russia, the term "droshky" was brought here by Russian-Jewish immigrants and referred to horse-drawn cabs.

The London cab trade is far older than the "'Ummingbird". In 1634 the first recognised cab rank was established at the Maypole Inn in the Strand by Captain Bailey, a member of Sir Walter Raleigh's expeditions. Twenty years later, Oliver Cromwell, ever anxious to control every aspect of English lives, brought in an Act of Parliament that set up The Fellowship of Master Hackney Carriages, licensing 200 cabbies.

That act makes the London cab the oldest regulated public transport system in the world. Today London's cabs are licensed by Transport for London.

The job has changed in the years I've been doing it. Transport for London has reduced the roads that cabs may traverse. There is more competition; the halcyon days of cabbies turning down work they didn't want are gone. Despite far more people using cabs and private hire than in the 1970s, they have more choice in the service.

We have trains that run all night, more buses than you could shake a stick at, rickshaws, bikes, apps like Uber and, if Google has its way, self-driving cabs, all chasing customers.

Driving a cab is an old man's game. According to statistics published by Transport for London in October 2018, there are three times more London cabbies over 60 than under 40. This statistic is reversed for registered private hire drivers. Sadly, with a total of 23,474 holding London cab licences, only 546 were women.

I must have travelled over three-quarters of a million miles driving a London cab, meeting passengers who have annoyed, bored, inspired, entertained and educated me in equal measure. I wouldn't change a thing, though: the passengers and London's rich history continually inspire me to write about this remarkable city.

David Styles has written about London on CabbieBlog.com since June 2008, which has been read by millions. He was Features Editor at Radio Taxis and plans to publish his memoir – Everyone is Entitled to my Opinion – *in 2022.* .

KNOW THE LINGO

Get up to speed with cabbies' code

Admirals – Dolphin Square, once notorious mansion blocks, due to their proximity to The Houses of Parliament, bearing the names of admirals.

All Nations – Cab shelter opposite Palace Gate near the Royal Albert Hall, close to where the Hall of Nations stood during the Great Exhibition of 1851.

Bilker – Not a member of Acker's jazz group of the Sixties, but someone who tries (and sometimes succeeds) in avoiding paying the fare for a journey – a not uncommon occurrence for the novice cabbie.

Butterboy – a new cabbie: you're new in the job and are "but a boy".

Confessional – The pull-down seat behind the driver.

Kipper Season – The time of year when business is a bit slack. Supposedly the term comes from when cabbies could only afford to eat kippers instead of steak.

PG Tips – Palace Gardens Terrace in Notting Hill, from the brand of tea with the same initials.

The Resistance – Harley Street, because doctors opposed the formation of the NHS.

Images: Shutterstock, Alamy, Régis Grman, Acabashi (CC BY-SA 4.0)

INTO THE COLD

Over seas of snow and by icy moonlight, Lin Bensley leads us through English literature's finest winters

LORNA DOONE

Wild ponies on Exmoor

All our house was quite snowed up, except where we had purged a way, by dint of constant shovellings. The kitchen was as dark and darker than the cider-cellar, and long lines of furrowed scollops ran even up to the chimney-stacks. Several windows fell right inwards, through the weight of the snow against them; and the few that stood, bulged in, and bent like an old bruised lanthorn. We were obliged to cook by candle-light; we were forced to read by candle-light; as for baking, we could not do it, because even the oven was too chill; and a load of faggots only brought a little wet down the sides of it . . . That night such a frost ensued as we never dreamed of, neither read in ancient books, or histories of Frobisher. The kettle by the fire froze, and the crock upon the hearth-cheeks; many men were killed, and cattle rigid in their head-ropes. Then I heard that fearful sound, which never had I heard before, neither since have heard (except during that same winter), the sharp yet solemn sound of trees burst open by frost-blow. Our great walnut lost three branches, and has been dying ever since; though growing meanwhile, as the soul does. And the ancient oak at the cross was rent, and many score of ash trees.

From *Lorna Doone* (1869) by R.D. Blackmore

Young John Ridd vows to avenge his father after he is attacked and murdered by the villainous Doone clan, who live amid the wilds of Exmoor. Set in the 17th century, Richard Doddridge Blackmore always maintained that *Lorna Doone* was a romantic story and not a historical novel, but in truth it is as much concerned with political intrigue and the avaricious machinations of our hero's adversaries as it is with affairs of the heart. One of the novel's many strengths is Blackmore's accurate portrayal of the Great Frost of December 1683, which lasted through to the end of April the following year.

Blackmore began his literary life writing volumes of verse before publishing his debut novel, *Clara Vaughan* – now regarded as one of the first examples of British detective fiction – though it was his third novel, *Lorna Doone*, that brought him fame and lasting success.

STOUR SEASONS

The first icicle of the season jabs from the guttering, a kind of black-white spike pointing to the earth. I scoop snow from a trough and scatter "wild bird seed", which is what it says on the label. There now, I tell myself, I have done my bit. I have shown true regret for not taking matins, and I have fed the hungry. And I am enjoying, at long range, the happiness of the season. And the white cat on the sill wears a nimbus of snowy sunshine, and wisely declines an invitation to go out.

In Good King Charles's winter days, even the court joined the sliders on the Thames. The river was almost solid ice, and people lit bonfires on it, built temporary shops on it, skated to the sea or to Oxford on it. The big thing was to roast an ox on it. Many people in villages or towns perished from the cold, of course. They were called the poor. Many people, young and old, were exhilarated by the sharpness of life, not death. Walk carefully. See the briefly transformed view. And as the Revd Sydney Smith advised, "Keep good fires."

From *Stour Seasons* (2016) by Ronald Blythe

Blythe is perhaps best known for his faithful evocation of Suffolk life in *Akenfield – Portrait of an English Village* (1969) – later adapted for film by Peter Hall – and which endures as one of the most perceptive and unsentimental accounts of rural life written in the 20th century. A champion of the poet John Clare, Blythe has also written other books that capture England. *Stour Seasons* is an object lesson in observation.

Basking in snowy sunshine . . .

Georgie Henley as Lucy in the 2005 film

THE LION, THE WITCH AND THE WARDROBE

Lucy felt a little frightened, but she felt inquisitive and excited as well. She looked back over her shoulder and there, between the dark tree-trunks, she could still see the open doorway of the wardrobe and even catch a glimpse of the empty room from which she had set out. (She had, of course, left the door open, for she knew that it is a very silly thing to shut oneself into a wardrobe.) It seemed to be still daylight there. "I can always get back if anything goes wrong," thought Lucy. She began to walk forward, crunch-crunch, over the snow and through the woods towards the other light.

In about ten minutes she reached it and found it was a lamp-post. As she stood looking at it, wondering why there was a lamp-post in the middle of a wood and wondering what to do next, she heard the pitter patter of feet coming towards her. And soon after that a very strange person stepped out from among the trees into the light of the lamp-post.

He was only a little taller than Lucy herself and he carried over his head an umbrella, white with snow. From the waist upwards he was like a man, but his legs were shaped like a goat's (the hair on them was glossy black) and instead of feet he had goat's hoofs.

From *The Lion, the Witch and the Wardrobe* (1950) by C.S. Lewis

The first in the *Chronicles of Narnia* series by Clive Staples Lewis remains the most popular and best known of all seven. Under the reign of the White Witch, Narnia is kept in a state of perpetual winter. Its one true ruler, Aslan (the original Lion King), has been absent for many years. None other than the Sons of Adam and Daughters of Eve can fulfil the prophecy and put an end to the Hundred Year Winter.

Lewis was a close friend of J.R.R. Tolkien and together they formed The Inklings: an informal literary discussion group who used to meet at The Eagle and Child pub in Oxford. The pair encouraged each other's writings, and Lewis dedicated his theological novel *The Screwtape Letters* (1942) to Tolkien, who played a leading role in his conversion to Christianity.

THROUGH THE WOODS

Snow, next to flowers and sunshine and perhaps the rainbow, is the loveliest of all natural events, certainly the loveliest of all winter happenings, lovelier than frost or winter moonlight. And in England it comes seldom enough to be a rare joy and never lingers long enough to be wearisome. It falls and performs its brief white miracle of transformation and vanishes again before the senses have grown used to that amazing whiteness . . .

I am not talking now of the snow which falls in towns, and which is not at all the most lovely winter phenomenon, but probably the most depressing and most hated: only of snow which falls in the country, opening out in a wonderful way its distances, creating a feeling of great light and tranquil spaciousness in its open fields and a strange softness and silence in its woods, the trees never moving under the weight of snow, the bird life suspended except for the dainty pattering of pheasants among bracken and bramble and over snow-sprinkled chestnut leaves and the wild cry of a mad blackbird escaping through the hazels. There is no stillness in the world like the stillness of the world under snow.

From *Through the Woods* (1936) by H.E. Bates

Winter's breathtaking wide skies

It is evident from the opening lines of *Through the Woods* that Bates has an all-consuming passion for Mother Nature as he leads us into his woodland world, wherein he conveys the passage of the temperamental seasons from one April to the next.

After marrying, Bates settled at Little Chart Forstal in Kent, and it was here he wrote *Through the Woods*, a collection of penetrative essays describing the broad-leaved copse that ran beside a bend in the road just below his house and prompted so many of his meditations upon nature.

Images: Shutterstock, Alamy

Birds of a feather huddling together . . .

As a natural historian, birder, author and former TV producer behind such programmes as *Birding with Bill Oddie* and *Springwatch*, Stephen Moss ranks as one our most gifted and knowledgeable wildlife writers. After moving from London to the village of Mark on the Somerset Levels, Moss followed in the footsteps of that venerable parson/naturalist Gilbert White by charting the fortunes of the wildlife within the bounds of his own parish over the course of a year.

Wild Hares and Hummingbirds bears more than favourable comparison to White's *The Natural History of Selborne*, and for those seeking the mutual benefits that connecting with nature can offer, even in the coldest months, it is nothing less than essential reading.

WILD HARES AND HUMMINGBIRDS

Overnight, an unexpected, silent visitor has come to the village. Powering southwards down the length of England, across the Cotswold and Mendip Hills, it reached here in the early hours. As dawn breaks, we open our curtains to a landscape transformed into a sea of white. Our village, the county and the whole country have come to a standstill, in the worst winter weather for 30 years.

The village children can hardly believe their luck. A cheery local radio announcer confirms what they all hope to hear: school has been cancelled. And every child, in every home, has undergone a miraculous transformation. Clothes have been pulled on, breakfasts eaten up, and coats, boots and gloves donned with joyful enthusiasm. They can hardly wait to get out of the door – not for their lessons, but to play with an unfamiliar and exciting substance: snow.

With the snow still falling, all is silent. Apart from the occasional sparrow's chirp from the hedgerow along the lane, I hear nothing. The birds are far too busy to think of anything other than finding something to eat. If they fail to do so they will die – and soon. Cold weather on its own will not kill birds, but snow does: for it covers up their food supplies. So the arrival of this white blanket from the north is very bad news indeed.

From *Wild Hares and Hummingbirds* (2011) by Stephen Moss

CHRISTMAS AT COLD COMFORT FARM

It was Christmas Eve. Dusk, a filthy mantle, lay over Sussex when the Reverend Silas Hearsay, Vicar of Howling, set out to pay his yearly visit to Cold Comfort Farm. Earlier in the afternoon he feared he would not be Guided to go there, but then he had seen a crate of British Port-type wine go past the Vicarage on the grocer's boy bicycle, and it could only be going, by that road, to the farmhouse. Shortly afterwards he was Guided to go, and set out upon his bicycle.

The Starkadders, of Cold Comfort Farm, had never got the hang of Christmas, somehow, and on Boxing Day there was always a run on the Howling Pharmacy for lint, bandages, and boracic powder. So the Vicar was going up there, as he did every year, to show them the ropes a bit. (It must be explained that these events took place some years before the civilizing hand of Flora Poste had softened and reformed the Farm and its rude inhabitants.)

After removing two large heaps of tussocks which blocked the lane leading to the Farm and thereby releasing a flood of muddy, icy water over his ankles, the Vicar wheeled his machine on towards the farmhouse, reflecting that those tussocks had never fallen there from the dung-cart of Nature. It was clear that someone did not want him to come to the place. He pushed his bicycle savagely up the hill, muttering.

From *Christmas at Cold Comfort Farm* (1940) by Stella Gibbons

A photogenic ewe on the South Downs, Sussex

In *Cold Comfort Farm* (1932), journalist and author Stella Gibbons lampooned those rustic novels then in-vogue by the likes of Sheila Kaye-Smith and Mary Webb that one critic termed the "soil and gloom" genre. *Cold Comfort Farm* is the home of the dysfunctional Starkadder family and the matriarchal Aunt Ada Doom; a repressed baggage of irrational fears and inbred ignorance, all of whom fall prey to the civilising ploys of cousin Flora.

Gibbons' finely nuanced parody would prove to be her most popular work, though many of her subsequent novels warrant investigation. On occasion she returned to her comic alma mater in winter as demonstrated by the extract from the short story reproduced here.

This Bull was the inspiration for the Bull in The Archers. What's the beer called?

HM Elizabeth II meeting Michael Greco and Pam St Clement at which EastEnders' *pub?*

Cheers! The PM at the Coronation Street *pub, called?*

PUB QUIZ

How well do you know our English pubs? Kevin Young puts your knowledge to the test

1. What is the most common pub name in England?

2. Who claims to be Britain's oldest brewer?

Which famous person or people is or are associated with the following pubs?

3. The Grafton Arms, Westminster

4. The Eagle and Child, Oxford

5. The Eagle, Cambridge

6. The Blind Beggar, Whitechapel

7. Ye Olde Cheshire Cheese, off Fleet Street, London

8. There are five London Underground stations which are said to be named after pubs. What are they?

9. When was the pub smoking ban introduced in England?

10. When and where was the first gastropub opened?

11. Approximately how many pubs are there in England to the nearest 5,000?

12. How many have closed in the last 20 years? – 10 per cent, 15 per cent or 25 per cent?

13. Which 2013 Simon Pegg film featured an alien invasion and a pub crawl?

14. Which TV chef was brought up in a pub in Essex?

15. Which pub is mentioned in the nursery rhyme *Pop Goes the Weasel*?

16. Which common pub name commemorates a 1651 event after the Battle of Worcester?

17. Which pub won *The Good Pub Guide*'s Pub of the Year in 2021?

18. Which organisation was founded on 16 March 1971 in Kruger's Bar in Dunquin, Kerry, Ireland?

Soap bars: can you name the fictional pubs in these programmes?

19. *Coronation Street*

20. *EastEnders*

21. *Emmerdale*

22. *Heartbeat*

23. What beer is the preferred tipple in The Bull at Ambridge, favourite pub on *The Archers*?

24. What is the difference between keg and cask beer?

25. The title is much disputed, but which pub does the *Guinness Book of World Records* recognise as the oldest in England?

26. Which traditional pub game has 9 holes and 3 pegs?

27. Where is the highest pub in England?

Name the literary work(s) in which these fictional pubs appear:

28. The Boar's Head

29. The Prancing Pony

30. The Admiral Benbow Inn

31. The George and Vulture

32. The Duke Of Burgundy pub featured in which 1949 classic British comedy film?

33. Which pub, built on the site of a disused airfield in Martlesham, Suffolk, is named after a famous pilot who served there?

34. Which famous politician, who campaigned for wartime abstinence, said "We are fighting Germany, Austria and Drink, and as far as I can see the greatest of these three deadly foes is Drink"?

35. A 1935 invention by chemist Ted Leggatt and pub owner Frank Dabbs has probably saved many pub drinkers from injury. What was it?

Answers on page 106

Images: Shutterstock and Alamy

THE BOY KING

100 years on, Tallulah Rushaya considers an English aristocrat and archaeologist's most daring discovery

ON 26 November, 1922, archaeologist Howard Carter and keen Egyptologist George Herbert, 5th Earl of Carnarvon, were on the brink of the greatest Valley of the Kings excavation in history: King Tutankhamun's tomb. After six years, the duo had almost given up, but Carter persuaded Carnarvon to hold on for one more season. As they prepared to enter where no-one had gone for over 3,000 years, Howard Carter peered through the incision. "Can you see anything?" inquired Lord Canarvon, to which Carter replied excitedly, "Yes, wonderful things."

Ancient Egypt has long evoked an air of mystery and desert romance. Born circa 1341 BC, Tutankhamun, the Boy King, ascended the throne at the tender age of nine, ruling until his death, due to a chariot accident that caused a leg infection, at around the age of 18. During his reign, with the guidance of Grand Vizier Ay, he revived lost traditions and arts and restored temples. He also moved the royal court back to the city of Thebes, gripped all those long years ago by a determination to preserve Egypt's heritage.

Although Tutankhamun's tomb itself was humbler than other royal tombs, it still revealed an emporium of treasures. More than 5,000, in fact, were meticulously recorded by Carter: chariots, a throne, remains of food and wine. Inside a stone sarcophagus were three coffins, the innermost made of gold and gemstones. Inside lay the mummy of Tutankhamun. The death mask is now in the Cairo Museum. According to the current Lady Carnarvon, Fiona, one of the duo's most treasured findings was a painted chest, a replica of which is exhibited at Highclere Castle, in their permanent Egypt Exhibition.

After securing the tomb with a steel gateway, the first object was removed using a wooden stretcher and fastened with bandages. Larger objects proved more challenging, especially the animal couches and chariots, which had to be disassembled. The more items uncovered, the brighter the limelight grew, which Carter found rather embarrassing. The droves of visitors attracted to the Valley of the Kings worried him, but he was delighted when Lord Carnarvon placed the story in *The Times*.

Lord Carnarvon was "generous both in spirit and in money, donating many artworks to the British Museum," Lady Fiona says. "He appreciated the legacy of sharing, understanding it was the first excavation of its kind."

Carter was more stubborn, a perfectionist and often irascible. Nevertheless, both had been involved in precarious voyages, and shared a deep respect for Egypt. Their working relationship came to an end only a few months after their discovery, when Lord Carnarvon died in Egypt in 1923 from accidentally shaving an infected mosquito bite. Rumours began to circulate of the "Curse of the Pharaohs" for disturbing a king even though Carter, who spent his later years as a collector, lived until the age of 64, dying in 1939.

Carter and Carnarvon's legacy continues. Artefacts from the tomb have been exhibited all over the world, most recently in England at the Saatchi Gallery, London. Even they would most likely struggle to fathom just how important their discovery remains 100 years on. Not just for archaeology but us all, opening up the vast and lavish world of Ancient Egypt.

Howard Carter and an assistant examine Tutankhamun, in the 1920s

Tutankhamun's gold mask

Images: Shutterstock

QUIZ ANSWERS

CHOCOLATE QUIZ ANSWERS FROM PAGE 21

1. Terry Brook **2.** "It's not for girls"
3. Desperation, Pacification, Expectation, Acclamation, Realisation **4.** Dairy Milk
5. *In the Air Tonigh*t – Phil Collins
6. Wonka's Whipple-Scrumptious Fudgemallow Delight **7.** Joseph Rowntree
8. 3 Musketeers Bar **9.** Marathon
10. 25p **11.** J.M. Barrie's play of the same name
12. Dream **13**. 1971
14. Have a break. **15.** Dawn French
16. Thorntons **17.** Menier Chocolate Factory
18. Bournville **19.** "Get Some Nuts"
20. Maltesers

Identify the chocolate . . .

21. Toffee Crisp
22. Mars Bar
23. Boost
24. Double Decker
25. Topic
26. Snickers

A RIGHT ROYAL QUIZ ANSWERS FROM PAGE 56

1. William the Conqueror **2.**1900 **3.** 21
4. Under a car park in Leicester **5.** Adelaide
6. George VI **7.** August **8.** Captain Mark Phillips
9. George V in 1932 **10.** University of St Andrews
11. a – Edward I **12.** c – The Tower of London
13. c - Nine **14.** a – Jane Seymour
15. c – 17 Bruton Street, London
16. a – William IV aged 64 years 10 months
17. b – Fotheringhay Castle
18. a – Norman Hartnell
19. a – Claire Foy **20.** b – Edward VII
21. Lady Jane Grey – 9 days **22.** George II
23. Charles II **24.** Four: William II, Edward V, Edward VI, Elizabeth I **25.** Auxiliary Territorial Service **26.** Elizabeth I **27.** 14 **28.** Stephen
29. Princess Charlotte of Cambridge
30. Princess Margaret's, 1960
31. True **32.** False **33.** False – the Queen is the only member of the Royal Family who is not permitted to vote. Other members of the Royal Family could vote but choose not to. **34.** True **35.** False **36.** False
37. True **38.**True **39.** True **40.** True

WHERE IN ENGLAND QUIZ ANSWERS FROM PAGE 72

1. Lancashire **2.** Guildford **3.** Lancaster **4.** Cornwall **5.** The Isle of Wight **6.** Birmingham **7.** Lincolnshire **8.** Hereford **9.** Buckinghamshire **10.** Carlisle **11.** Northamptonshire, Buckinghamshire, Bedfordshire, Cambridgeshire and Norfolk **12.** Bristol **13.** Woodstock **14.** Felixstowe

PUB QUIZ ANSWERS FROM PAGE 104

1. The Red Lion **2.** Shepherd Neame **3.** The Goons; some of the early scripts were written there
4. "The Inklings" who included J.R.R. Tolkien and C.S. Lewis **5.** Francis Crick and James Watson, the discoverers of DNA **6.** The Kray Twins; Ronnie committed a murder there in 1966 **7.** Samuel Johnson (reputedly) and Charles Dickens **8.** Angel, Elephant & Castle, Manor House, Royal Oak and Swiss Cottage **9.** July 2007 **10.** 1991, The Eagle pub in Clerkenwell, London **11.** 40,000 **12.** 25 per cent
13. The World's End **14.** Jamie Oliver **15.** The Eagle on City Road, London **16.** The Royal Oak (where the future Charles II hid after the battle) **17.** The Olive Branch in Clipsham Rutland **18.** CAMRA, the Campaign for Real Ale **19.** The Rovers Return
20. The Queen Vic **21.** The Woolpack
22. The Aidensfield Arms **23.** Shires Ale
24. Cask beer is unfiltered and naturally carbonated by secondary fermentation. Keg beer is filtered and artificially carbonated. **25.** Ye Olde Fighting Cocks in St Albans, Hertfordshire **26.** Bar billiards
27. Tan Hill Inn in North Yorkshire at 1,732 feet (528m)
28. *Henry IV parts I* and *II* **29.** *The Lord of the Rings*
30. *Treasure Island* **31.** *The Pickwick Papers*
32. *Passport to Pimlico* **33.** Douglas Bader
34. David Lloyd George, 1915
35. The modern sisal dartboard – it replaced the solid blocks of wood which were previously used.

A BRIEF HISTORY OF THIS ENGLAND

WHEN *This England* was first sent out into the world 54 years ago, editor Roy Faiers vowed the magazine would, "Instead of politics . . . bring you the poetry of the English countryside in words and pictures. Instead of bigotry we shall portray the beauty of our towns and villages. Instead of prejudice there will be pride in our ancient traditions, the surviving crafts, the legends, the life, the splendour and peace of this England."

In these divisive times, this sentiment remains true. In the face of adversity, we strive to create a magazine that will provide respite amidst chaos. In the last 12 months at *This England*, we have remained true to our slogan, "as refreshing as a pot of tea". It has been a year of blending old with new, taking a nostalgic look at the past and celebrating modern England.

Our much-loved *Royal History* series came to a close after 15 years. It was with a bang that the wonderful Paul James rounded off the series, with memorable features on HM the Queen and the late great Duke of Edinburgh.

Our *My England* segment was privileged to feature wise words from Captain Sir Tom Moore in what was, sadly, one of his last

The first cover of This England

interviews, as well as legendary dambuster Johnny Johnson.

Those seeking light relief were not disappointed with Brian Viner's column, as he continued to get to grips with modern Britain, from pet tortoises to a Peloton bike. We have you, our readers, to thank for the poetry which came to the fore in *Poets' Corner*.

Finally, we hope celebrating our churches brought some solace. The past year has seen some true gems – our favourite being St Just in Roseland, Cornwall, ensconced in its tropical gardens.

Explore England returned in March 2021, whisking us off to the tranquil Forest of Bowland, and the healing beauty of Kiftgate's Court Gardens in the Cotswolds, to name just two. There was a weekend in Windsor and a look at Oxford's Bodleian Library following John Thaw who roamed the city in *Inspector Morse*.

In this year's *Annual*, enjoy our events pages. From the age-old Chelsea Flower Show to the Grimaldi Clown Service, if it's happening in England, you'll find it here! Look out for our English Bridges features, highlighting some of our country's fascinating architecture. If you want to test your knowledge, we have quizzes on everything from English geography to royalty to the nation's best-loved chocolates.

In honour of her Platinum Jubilee, we celebrate Her Majesty's life in pictures. Chris Franks reflects on the history of Wimbledon, while Linda Barrett meets the superstars of the RAF – the Red Arrows. Gillian Thornton discovers Hertfordshire's horticultural heroes, Rebecca Franks celebrates Ralph Vaughan Williams' *The Lark Ascending* on the 150th anniversary of his birth, and James Hulme takes us on a journey over England's railways.

We hope our 2022 *Annual* gives you a taste of the diverse content you can find in every issue of *This England*. If we've piqued your interest, you can find information about subscriptions overleaf.

The quarterly issues of This England are every bit as enjoyable as this annual edition; in fact even more so! Each quarterly issue of This England magazine celebrates England's countryside, customs, history and heritage accompanied by beautiful seasonal photographs. It also has a lively letters page, with readers exchanging views and sharing memories on all sorts of subjects.

This England is cherished by readers far and wide but it's not always easy to get hold of a copy in the shops. With a subscription you can be sure to receive each seasonal issue. Subscribe today and get your first issue for only £1, that's just £16 for the whole year, with free UK delivery direct to your door. When you take out a direct debit or 2 year pre-paid subscription you'll also receive one of our stunning Country Calendars absolutely FREE, worth £6.50.

Angela Linforth

Angela Linforth, Editor

GREAT REASONS TO SUBSCRIBE...

- **SAVE OVER 80%** on the shop price via Direct Debit — only £16 for one year.
- **FREE** greetings card available, on request, with each gift subscription.
- **FREE** This England Country Calendar when you pay by direct debit or take out a 2 or 3 year pre-paid subscription, worth £6.50.
- **FREE** UK delivery, direct to your door.
- **GUARANTEED** lowest price direct from the publisher.
- **NEVER MISS** an issue.

BEST DEAL DIRECT DEBIT	1 YEAR PREPAY	2 YEAR PREPAY
ONLY £16.00 First issue £1 then £5 per quarter thereafter.	~~£22.00~~ £19.80	~~£41.80~~ £37.62
SAVE 82% +FREE calendar	SAVE 10%	SAVE 10% +FREE calendar

ALSO AVAILABLE AS A DIGITAL SUBSCRIPTION

Why not try This England as a digital subscription and read your issues on the go? Available to buy on the App Store and Google Play.

Available on the App Store | ANDROID APP ON Google play | Buy Digital Subscription

IT'S EASY TO SUBSCRIBE:

CALL: **0800 074 0188** Quoting code: **ANN22**

(Free from UK landlines and mobiles) Mon-Fri 8am-6pm. Overseas: +44 1382 575052